Get Back on that Horse

Using Hypnosis and NLP to
Get Over Your Fear of Riding

Thomas Mulryne

Get Back on that Horse

Using Hypnosis and NLP to Get Over Your Fear of Riding

www.EquestrianHypnoCoach.com

All rights reserved. No part of this book may be reproduced or transmitted in any form or by any means, electronic or mechanical, including photocopying, recording, or by any information storage and retrieval system without the permission of the publisher.

Disclaimer

This book is not intended as a substitute for psychotherapy, coaching, or counseling, nor should it be used to diagnose or treat any medical or psychological condition. The reader should consult a physician or therapist in matters related to personal health. This book is intended to provide information and education to the reader. Neither the author, the editors, nor the publisher shall be held liable for any physical, psychological, emotional, relational, financial, or spiritual outcomes. The stories in this book are based on real situations though the names and all personal identifying information have been altered to protect identity.

First Printing: 2023

Published by Equestrian Hypno Coach Publications

Copyright © 2023 by Thomas Mulryne

First Edition

ISBN 979-8-9884329-0-6

About the Author

I began my athletic career early and participated in many sports. I know firsthand the feeling of entering the batter's box or walking up to the free throw line with the game on the line and the fate of my team resting squarely on my shoulders. Standing on the pool's edge, waiting for the official to blow the whistle and start the race, I wondered if I was as good or fast as the swimmer two lanes over.

And I clearly remember like it was yesterday showing my horse, and as we approached the jump, the closer we got, the higher the jump seemed to get. That top rail got a little higher and a little more daunting with each stride. I was trying to hide my nervousness and uncertainty, sure that if my horse picked up my shaken confidence, he might balk and refuse the jump and possibly send me airborne onto the show ring dirt.

Despite spending countless hours practicing and preparing for competition, my daydreams of cheering fans and fantasies of stardom were rarely realized. It was never a question of me not doing enough to get in shape, hone my skills, or work my horse to prepare him for competition. I was always driven, always determined to succeed. Over time, I came to realize that if I only had more confidence and more belief in myself and my abilities, if I could somehow find a way to get rid of my anxiety, calm my nerves, and play without thoughts like "Don't blow it" or "Don't choke," then I might be able to execute when it counted, under pressure!

I couldn't even imagine there might be a way to take control of my thoughts.

After raising three girls (who have blessed me with five grandchildren), I am acutely aware of how quickly time flies and how precious time really is. I don't want to see them or my grandkids or anyone's children not realize their potential or, worse, develop destructive beliefs from their failure to achieve their goals. The lessons we learn from competing in sports are instrumental in shaping our lives.

I now really appreciate and understand how important playing sports was to me as well as it was to my kids.

I was bitten by the horse bug from the tender age of nine. From the moment I first rode at a local hack stable where they offered trail rides, I knew that this was something I wanted more of in my life, and it was not long after that I became one of the "barn kids" who worked at the barn taking care of the sixty plus horses stabled there simply for the opportunity to ride. We would saddle up the customers' mounts and then hop on our own, bareback, and lead the trail rides. On busy summer days, there were times when spending eight hours on horseback was not an unusual occurrence. I spent a lot of time at that barn and worked my way up the pecking order until I became the top rider. That meant whenever a new horse was purchased, I would be the first to jump on to see what they would do. Some were not all that well broke, so you had better have some skills to ride without being thrown off.

When I was fifteen, I purchased my own horse, Golden Nugget, a well-trained palomino stallion who was a dream to ride. We did some local shows, and he was so well-balanced and collected that he never failed to switch leads, and we would take home the blue ribbon in almost every class we entered.

In 1976, I took a semester off from college to enroll in a farrier training program, and later that year, I started a farrier business. Shortly after that, I was lucky to find a highly skilled craftsman who showed me the fine points of shoeing racehorses. I have learned very well how to deal with pressure, and I'm not just talking about building a successful business. Eventually, I was able to work for some of the biggest names in racing on some of the top horses in the sport, where millions of dollars could be on the line. And with that kind of money comes a load of stress. You see, these trainers cannot afford to have anything go wrong that might interfere with their horse's performance. I had to figure out how to deal with the responsibilities that come with the job and, over time, learned to even enjoy the pressure!

I had always been interested in what made people tick, even before I studied psychology at the university. I was first introduced to neuro-linguistic programming (NLP) in the late 1980s and studied various training programs in NLP and hypnosis since then. When I realized that I could not keep up with the physical demands that shoeing horses takes on my body forever, I answered my second calling in life and jumped in with both feet to learn all that I could about change work. After receiving multiple certifications in NLP, humanistic neuro-linguistic psychology, hypnosis, and coaching, I realized that what I enjoyed most was helping people with performance enhancement. I became a certified mental toughness trainer, which was geared primarily toward athletic performance. I also became certified in several different sports performance protocols. I work with athletes and performers in several contexts, including actors, musicians, sales, academics, and public speaking. Due to my lifelong experience in the horse world, many of my clients come from here. I enjoy working with competitive riders and those who, for whatever reason, have developed a fear of riding. You can learn more about what I do by visiting my websites:

www.MentalSportsCoach.com
www.EquestrianHypnocoach.com
www.GetInZone.com

My life was going great, better than I ever could have dreamed of, and I thought I had everything well sorted out and had all the answers when a loved one fell prey to addiction. This rocked my world, and I tried to do everything I could to stop it. Yet despite all my best efforts and well-thought-out ideas on how to get them off the path of self-destruction they were traveling on, nothing was working. I have never been so terrified or felt so helpless and powerless in my life.

Let's just say a whole lot of things happened that were difficult to deal with, and throughout it all, I was hell-bent on trying to change things. I could not just sit by and watch my loved one play on the tracks watching out for, waiting for, and just knowing that the train was coming, and I just had to stop it. I had to do something to get them to turn things around. I was absolutely driven to do something before it became too late to save them.

And on my hands and knees, eventually, I found my way to a twelve-step group filled with people just like me who could not stop someone they loved from giving up a problem that might kill them. And I learned many, many things from those people. Ordinary people who had been going down that same painful road that I was on, who were a little wiser than I was, and who were kind enough to take that wisdom that they had already learned from their pain and suffering, shared their experiences with me. Here I was, a man who was old enough to have it all figured out and knew exactly what needed to be done to navigate through life successfully, and I suddenly found out that all that I thought I already knew to be true was, in reality, just an illusion.

All along, I had simply gotten very, very lucky.

I was not in control of all that much and certainly not in control of anyone else. Eventually, by the grace of God, my loved one found their way out of that hole and found for themselves a much better way to live. My behavior had nothing to do with it. My loved one is the one who did it because, after all, they were the only one who could. I learned that everything can change in the blink of an eye and sometimes for the best.

And so I continued to go to meetings, and as someone now armed with a little more experience and maybe even a little more wisdom, I eventually gave others some of the gifts that were so freely given to me. I discovered the pure joy that comes from helping ease another person's pain. I realized how good I feel when I am fortunate enough to ease their suffering. I now know the ecstasy (and I really can't come up with a better word to describe it) that I feel when I can help someone else deal with a problem that they have struggled with. These wonderful emotions and feelings transcend the search for money.

Certainly, we all need some money to survive and prosper, but what I learned, and perhaps it was the greatest gift of all that I received from my experiences with addiction, was how great it is to help someone in need. This is what has set me on this new path in life—a new calling—to help other people deal with their problems and to enable them to lead happier, more successful, more prosperous, and more rewarding lives. Who better to help than young people because they have their whole lives ahead of them? Whether they go through life afraid of failure or fearless makes all the difference!

So many people go through life afraid. They are so afraid that often they don't even try. And I just find that so very tragic. It's heartbreaking.

I decided to direct my energy toward helping young people learn how to achieve their goals in their sport and, even more importantly, in their lives.

I discovered a system that really works and can solve the problems that so many athletes struggle with, whether it is a lack of confidence or pressure that prevents them from performing in competition as well as they do in practice or whether they ask themselves, "Am I good enough?" This system answers these questions and solves these problems. The methods contained in it have already helped thousands of people improve by making them aware of what is happening inside their heads and, even more importantly, exactly what to do about it and how to bring their best game onto the field. And with the knowledge gained from this program and armed with the techniques and skills you get from learning them, you can go beyond the world of sports and help your child lead more prosperous, fulfilling, and successful lives. This really pumps me up, and I am excited by the thought of helping them excel in their sport and beyond! Let's do this!

Table of Contents

Introduction 1

CHAPTER 1: Falling in Love Again 7

CHAPTER 2: Intention 17

CHAPTER 3: Thoughts and Thinking 27

CHAPTER 4: Emotional Mastery 43

CHAPTER 5: Seeing and Hearing 53

CHAPTER 6: Neuro-Linguistic Programming 65

CHAPTER 7: Hypnosis 77

CHAPTER 8: Biological Response 89

CHAPTER 9: Choices 99

Resources 107

Introduction

Allow me to start my story by sharing that I was initially bitten by the horse bug at a young age, which is to say that I was first drawn towards and then fell in love with horses by the age of ten. I spent a good deal of my time during my teen years riding horses and being around the stables. From the beginning watching the farrier shoe horses always fascinated me. When the blacksmith came to the barn, I would hang around whenever I could, watching closely and trying to make myself useful by sweeping the floor or whatever else needed doing as he worked. I imagined myself learning how to do this work someday. I rode every chance I got, which was often, and when I was fifteen, I bought my own horse and paid for his board and feed with money that I earned from a newspaper route. He was a palomino stallion bred and trained at the King Ranch, which was at that time a famous breeding operation in Texas. The horse was well-trained and went by the name Golden Nugget. I rode him every day. Some of my fondest memories are being at that barn, riding him through those trails, and in the training ring. I took him to shows, and he performed well in the show ring because he was such a well-trained, balanced, and collected mover. We got our share of blue ribbons. The only downside was that he was a stallion, and because I was under eighteen years of age, I was not permitted to show him at the state fair, which was the biggest and most prestigious competition around. I also played many sports in those days, my favorite being basketball, and when I was not out riding, I could usually be found at the courts, shooting hoops.

Unfortunately, when I was seventeen, Nugget got colic and then jaundiced, and things got so bad we had to put him down. This broke my heart and I shied away from going to the barn after that happened because things were never quite the same after he was gone. Shortly after that, I went away to college, so I was not around horses all that much during that entire time. I was interested in and studied psychology while there. One day a few of us were hiking through the mountains near the school, and we came across a horse farm, and for some reason, it hit me how much I had really missed that part of my life.

When I finished school, I decided to learn how to shoe horses and enrolled in the Farrier program at Central Wyoming College in January of 1976. Outside of the people I befriended in the horse world, no one in my family had anything to do with horses. None of my friends, and because I grew up in a suburban, no one else in my entire high school owned a horse or even had anything to do with horses. When I announced that I would become a horseshoer, most of the people around me thought I was nuts. It was so foreign of a notion to them to even consider that there were people out there in the world who were still putting shoes on horses, let alone making a living.

A few friends cracked jokes about it, but most people in my world just rolled their eyes when they first heard my plans. For some unexplainable reason, this lack of support only made me want it even more. After completing the Farrier program, I came back east and tried to start a business trimming and shoeing horses. I got married that summer, and we moved into a little house on a farm where they trained Standardbreds, harness racing horses. Because it was a struggle building up my farrier business, I got a job at the farm and began to learn how to take care of racehorses. I always made it a point of being around whenever the farrier came out to shoe at the barn. After about a year or so, I was able to talk my way into an apprenticeship position with the horseshoer, Charles Nesbitt, who was accomplished as a master farrier. I followed him to the racetracks, and under his tutelage, my skills improved dramatically. This set me up to enjoy a successful career that spanned close to five decades.

Along the way, a racetrack farrier friend of mine, Norman LeClair, introduced me to a very new thing called Neuro-Linguistic Programming or NLP, which some people in California developed. I will explain what it is further along in the book. For now, let me say that NLP has many facets, but it is basically a study of how the mind works (neuro) combined with communication (linguistics), both in terms of human interactions as well as internally, which is to say the ways we break down sensory data or how we relate to the world (or how our mind is programmed). It has applications in human communication, regarding self-improvement, in sales and marketing, as well as in psychological therapeutic interventions or change work, people making changes on themselves, or in helping others to change (therapy). Anyway, this appealed to me because of my lifelong interest in psychology, but specifically, what most intrigued me was the work done in this field regarding rapport building. At that point in my life, being successful in my business so that I could make money was paramount to me. I was raising three daughters and was ambitious by nature.

Now the funny thing is, at that point, I was unaware of the relationship between NLP and hypnosis (they are very closely aligned). When my friend Norman decided to give up his farrier practice to become a hypnotist, I was convinced the poor boy had absolutely lost his marbles. As I delved deeper into the study, I began to see the correlation and the overlap between the two modalities. You see, I really had no idea what hypnosis was, but the more I read and studied, the more aware I became. And the more interested I became in the field of hypnosis. What makes this funny to me now is that after I learned enough and eventually decided to pursue a second career, becoming a professional hypnotist, I now cannot hold it against anyone who covertly rolls their eyes at me when I declare to them that I am a hypnotist. I laugh because that was my exact reaction when my friend Norman told me the very same thing. I understand where those people are coming from.

What I also find funny is how when I came out and told family and friends what I was up to, their reaction was not all that different than the reaction I received when deciding to become a horseshoer many years ago. My daughters thought it funny when they fashioned aluminum foil hats for themselves and my grandchildren so they would all somehow be protected from crazy Dad's hypnotic mental wavelengths. I get the joke! There have been a lot of analogous patterns that I have noticed between my journey as a horseshoer and my journey as a hypnotist, from the acquisition of some impactful mentors to the learning curve as well as the early experiences acquiring clients. It is hard for me not to notice history seemingly repeating itself in so many ways. There are some stark differences as well. Back when I was an aspiring and then a journeyman horseshoer, chasing and making money was a big motivational driver. Becoming a hypnotist has so much less to do with earning money and so much more to do with helping people than anything else. I am at a much different point in my life. I have been blessed in so many ways during my life. None of us will get out of this place alive, and the closer you get to the end, the more you tend to evolve as a person. Monetary self-advancement becomes less meaningful, while helping other people has become much more satisfying. I guess you could say selfishness gives way to selflessness. It is nice to be able to, on occasion, at least, notice some glimmers of evolvement shine through.

My interest in doing change work, whether as a hypnotist, a mental sports coach, or an NLP practitioner, has been centered on helping performers improve their performance. Whether it be a public speaker, in academics, or in a business context, it is good to know I can add value. What excites me is working with athletes largely because I know how much value I can add here, and I see the need for what I can offer. I can only wish I would have had someone like who I am now come into my life back when I was a youth competing in sports to help me navigate all that comes with being on that journey. Due to my lifelong association with the horse world and its people, it is always especially exciting to work with equestrians, whether those competing in dressage, equitation, jumping, western pleasure, or reining. And especially those who I am writing this book for. And I am speaking to those who have lost just a bit of their nerve for one reason or another and those who may begin to feel panic swell up in their gut at even the thought of cantering through a wide-open meadow. Do not despair, for there is help for you wherever you are right now. The reality is that the thought itself, more than anything else, has been stopping you. And I am certain that even if you have temporarily forgotten yourself, you are more powerful, much more powerful than any thought that happens to be passing through your mind. It really can be as simple as just being able to let go of a thought.

CHAPTER 1

Falling in Love Again

Karen spent a large part of her early years in stables and riding arenas, enjoying being in the company of ponies. Over time, she became a better-than-average, competent equestrian. She was first introduced to horseback riding when her cousins talked her into accompanying them on an excursion over to the local hack stable, where they signed up to ride one beautiful bright sunny day when she was nine. It truly was love at first sight. She instantly liked everything about the experience, from the saddle's squeak, the barn's smells, and the wind in her face as they rode through the woods and across fields and meadows. You could not wipe the smile off her face, and she just couldn't get enough after that first ride. She returned, again and again, that summer and wanted to do little else with her time from that point on. She talked to one of the kids that worked there leading the trail rides and was excited to learn that Roy, the owner enlisted the help of local kids who were willing to do the barn work in return for the opportunity to ride. By the following summer, she became one of those kids and thus began her journey into the world of horses.

She started off mucking stalls and feeding and watering the animals and, before long, learned how to correctly put on the saddle and bridle for the customers that came to ride. A more experienced hand would lead a group, and for bigger groups, another rider or two would go along to help anyone who had trouble controlling their mount during the hour-long ride. The stables housed about sixty horses and another twenty or so ponies, and the place got busy when the weather was good. Sometimes there might be up to an hour's wait before a group would saddle up and be led through the gate and out to the trails. Almost every one of the animals would get plenty of work, at least the ones that were quiet enough that you could depend on them not to hurt any of the typically inexperienced riders. The staff rode the more spirited ones, assigned according to the level of skill each rider had attained, and there were always a few horses that were still too fractious and untrained enough even to be trusted in the hands of the barn's top riders. Because things got so hectic during the peak times, the staff would not have time to tack up their own, so they would generally just slip on the bridle and ride bareback when taking out the groups. On some weekends, they might spend up to eight hours on horseback, with less than ten minutes helping customers dismount and getting the next group on board for the next ride.

During the winter months, after school, and on weekends when the weather was too cold and snowy for any customers to show up, the kids that worked there at the stables would take turns riding all the horses to get them some exercise.

Those horses that, in the summer when they were being worked hard, were lazy and docile, and it was a real struggle to get them to move faster than a walk, were a completely different ride on a cold winter day when they hardly ever got out of the barn. They would be quite the handful, quick to buck and spin and sometimes bolt and try to run off with you. Even an experienced rider on the top of their game might get tossed off occasionally. With all that time spent on horseback and the opportunity to ride all kinds of different horses, Karen and her friends became pretty good little riders over a relatively short time frame. She had spent a lot of time developing her riding skills over that eight to ten-year span working for Roy and was no rookie by the time life got in the way, and she no longer had the time to spend at the barn. She had developed some serious skills by the time she went to college, but from then on, her opportunities to ride just became less and less frequent. As time marched on, she became more focused on her job and career, and then marriage and raising the kids soon followed, and her time at the barn became no more than distant memories, some of her most cherished memories certainly.

Fast forward to the point in her life when Karen's children were grown and had gone their own way, busy with their own careers and families. Karen and her mate were now empty nesters, and while her husband kept himself plenty busy between work and a time-consuming golf habit, Karen found herself with plenty of time on her hands. All her life up until now, raising her kids as well as working at the school where she was employed had put crazy busy demands on her schedule, but all of that had now changed. She had often found herself reminiscing about her teen years as an avid rider and longed to rekindle the passion she had once felt so strongly and decided to buy herself a horse. This was the perfect time for her to do that, and the exercise that riding would provide would be a sweet bonus. She found herself a flashy little Quarter horse paint mare to buy and a stable not too far from her home where she could keep her.

It was a well-run barn operation where they did all the work, and all that Karen needed to do was simply show up and ride. There were quite a few boarders at the place and some right around her age. She soon became friends with a couple of them. The facility was near state land with hundreds of acres on which to ride and had both indoor and outdoor riding arenas and a couple of riding instructors who worked with those who wanted their help. Karen was surprised to find herself feeling awkward and even a little uncomfortable when she first started back riding. But she told herself it was probably natural that she would feel this way, considering it had been close to thirty years since her heyday as an equestrian. She expected that window of self-doubt and uncertainty would diminish quickly, and she would soon feel right at home being back in pretty good form before long. She had purchased a western saddle along with her mare and expected, after all those years riding a variety of different mounts bareback and without a saddle, that it would take no time at all to bond with and feel right at home aboard her horse Black Betty especially considering she now was riding with the comfort and sense of safety, having the luxury of riding with stirrups, a comfortable seat and even a saddle horn to grab onto should she feel the need to steady herself from time to time. It almost seemed like it would be hard to fall off while riding in western tack. Although she found Betty to be a sweet little horse for the most part, being only four years old and sold as being "green-broke," the mare was a little high-strung and could be a bit "spooky," especially on cooler days when the wind had a little bite to it after it picked up a bit.

After realizing that the feelings of apprehensiveness that she was experiencing were not diminishing quite as quickly as she had hoped, Karen decided to enroll in some riding classes with the hopes that it might help settle her nerves some and allow her time to find a more comfortable comfort zone whenever she was on Betty's back. Although her instructor, Ms. Evelyn, was clearly an accomplished equestrian, Karen was a little disappointed with the lessons. The focus was bent more strongly toward the more technical aspects of riding. Although there was nothing wrong with being reminded to keep her heels down and her body posture in alignment, Karen felt that her issues were a lot more on the mental side than the physical. Ms. Evelyn's prompts for her to "stay relaxed" and reminders that "your horse knows when you are tense, loosen up" were certainly well-intentioned but came up a bit short, and they were proved to be not all that helpful. Karen knew she needed to become more relaxed and looser and did not need someone to tell her what she already knew. She needed to find out exactly "how" to relax, and not just that she needed to relax. Over time she felt the instructor was becoming increasingly impatient and often felt as though she was being talked down to. She felt like she was not gaining all that much from the lessons, and rather than waste any more time and money, she decided to discontinue taking them and dropped out of class.

Karen knew that she was having difficulty relaxing, and she could clearly see that her horse was picking up her anxiety. Horses have a keen sixth sense, and their survival instincts are strongly connected with their ability to read the energy around them. Horses are prey animals vulnerable to the various predators that exist in the wild. It is ingrained in them as they travel through the world to be on the lookout and ever vigilant to any sign of trouble and alert to anything that might possibly be of danger to them. When a person around them shows even the slightest signs of nervousness, they cannot help but signal to the horse that this person is afraid, so there must be something to be afraid of. All of this will trigger the animal's own highly sensitive nervous system. "Uh oh, this person is afraid. Red alert! There must be something dangerous to be afraid of!" Of course, this is all happening inside the horse's mind on a nonverbal level, but this is, in effect, what is happening. Horses do not have the cognitive ability to use self-talk as a human does, but they are sensitive to what is going on around them. If the human is displaying even a hint of fear, the horse will be keenly aware and responsive to their energy.

Although Karen understands all of this even after being away from horses for so many years, and although she was once a very competent rider back in the day, her comfort zone has shrunk to the point that she suspects it may be gone completely. Knowing all of this does not make it any easier to let go of the thought in the back of her mind that any time her mount becomes startled, she could be caught off guard and the possibility that she could fall off her horse and get injured was a genuine and present danger. It is only natural for a woman now close to fifty to feel a lot more at risk than when she was fifteen. Teenagers think of themselves as being invincible. Most people are much more fearful of being injured as they age. After all, we don't bounce quite as high as we once did when we hit the ground. Bones become more brittle and more vulnerable to breaking, and the recovery time after an injury is likely to take longer, and the pain that comes with it will probably linger on as well. After being away from horses for three decades, it is a human reaction to feel tentative, apprehensive, and even downright scared to death of being hurt when they get back around horses. Certainly, it is natural to be more afraid than a teenager who has been spending all their free time and is used to being around horses all the time. So being afraid of being hurt physically is perfectly normal to be expected and legitimate. In many states, for insurance purposes, signs are posted all over the barn area warning that being around horses is inherently dangerous and you are coming onto the grounds at your own risk. A reason for this is that because horses are a lot bigger than humans, people can and sometimes get hurt.

All this being said, there is usually more than just the danger of being injured that causes a person to feel anxious while riding horses at play here. When you are riding in an arena like Karen is doing and other people are standing around watching you ride, the fear of being judged and embarrassed is sometimes the biggest factor causing consternation and discomfort. It is a funny thing that is often happening in the horse world. For many people, an unspoken dynamic is going on, and often this is happening beneath the surface of conscious awareness. Many people like to think of themselves as accomplished equestrians and often tend to overestimate their skill level, even to the point that they like to consider themselves an expert. There is rarely a shortage of these self-proclaimed know it all types hanging around the barnyards. And though they may not say it out loud, many are quite full of themselves and not at all hesitant to share exactly what they are doing wrong with the others around them. Often there is an unspoken rivalry when more than one of these people cross paths.

A rarely spoken out-loud "I know more than you do about horses" dynamic is often at play. Truthfully all of this is like the dominant broodmare thing going down in a paddock full of mares. When they first turn out together, there will be some serious kicking and maybe a bit of biting going on as well. Eventually, the pecking order will be established, and things will usually be settled from that point forward, except if the mares are all fed outside in different feed buckets. Then the dynamic may resurface again, and it is usually a given that one or two mares will get a few more mouthfuls of grain while the less aggressive may end up losing a few pounds of weight. The same dynamic plays out with the humans in the barns, though more subtly. There may be an occasional more overt example on display from time to time, but usually, most of this takes place on a much more passive-aggressive level. Now, this is not by any means an attempt to excuse typical alpha male dynamics that also is always in play in the human-animal rankings. It is just that stallions are usually never turned out together in the same field because no one wants to risk a blood bath and possible serious injury occurring, so the whole dynamic is typically only seen amongst a band of broodmares. The truth is that the more expert the level of horsemanship a person has attained, the less concerned they seem to be about where they place on the ladder of who is being ranked as the best. This is not unique to horse people. The best drummers, the best chefs, and the best baseball players in the world, although they may remain highly competitive, they are more apt to respect their peers, those that have reached the highest levels of a skill set, than they are to be concerned with wasting their energy over "I am better than you" thinking. In the horse world, many people get caught up in all this type of thinking. There tends to be a game of one-upmanship being played out, and all of this adds to the genuine fear which only takes place inside the heads of those afraid of being embarrassed by being judged as having less than adequate horsemanship abilities. In short, it is usually a combination of fear of physical injury along with a fear of being embarrassed that is at play here.

All of this may fall under the "good to know" category but not all that important. For many years the field of psychology was very concerned with the "why" question. If we can figure out why this person is afraid, and if we can go back in their history and determine exactly what initial sensitizing episode (ISE) caused this fear or phobia, then we can fix it. Now, on the surface, this seems to have some logic attached to it, and occasionally all of this could possibly be helpful. Still, over time many in the field have discovered that finding the answer to "why" the person behaves the way they do often has very little to do with helping them discover the resolution they are seeking. Finding the cause is often useless or at least less useful in figuring out the answer to the "how" (as in how to fix it) question. In Karen's case seeing "what" is going on (she is nervous) or "why" she became nervous is a lot less important in helping her know "how" to change the situation. If Karen's story resonates with you or anyone you know, it is not at all surprising because, in the real world, it is a very common scenario. It is very human to feel uncomfortable after spending a prolonged period away from the barns and horses. It is also not unusual for people to get a little rattled from time to time for all the reasons mentioned earlier. Once we fall out of our comfort zone and begin to let self-doubts creep in, these feelings tend to escalate if we do not address them in effective ways. As we progress through this book, I intend to provide you with many different strategies to help you overcome some of these challenges. Hopefully, along the way, I will be able to provide you with some useful answers to the "how do I do this" question in the hopes of giving you a chance to overcome what is now causing you to hesitate or even completely stop you from doing an activity that you once loved to engage in. I know that there are strategies that I will include in this book that have already helped others succeed. My purpose in writing this is to help you take the action you need to take to restore and rebuild your confidence levels so that you can enjoy more fully every minute that you get to spend in the company of and on top of the back of your horses.

CHAPTER 2

Intention

Before we get to the "how" questions, start with a couple of "what" questions, such as what is going on and what we want instead. The change process always starts with awareness, that is, paying attention to where you are presently and then really getting clear about where specifically you desire to end up. Many people go through life without giving much thought to these things. Life unfolds quickly, and without asking themselves questions that encourage them to slow down and take a good look at what is really happening, some will get caught up reacting to one thing and then just keep going on to the next thing that happens to them and then react to it, all the while remaining oblivious to what is really going on. Life seems just to be happening to them all the time, and like a leaf in a stream, they get carried along, oblivious to the fact that they are very powerful beings that are meant to choose what they want rather than merely accepting things as they are. Over time it tends to become their default position to live this way. Most of us have no clue as to just how powerful we really are. We are more powerful than we think, more powerful than we are even able to think or even imagine. Regardless of how powerful the current is in the stream of life, it is our birthright to decide to put a paddle in the river and determine for ourselves which direction our lives will take. Often, people get stuck in a pattern of just going along with what is, never thinking it is within their power to assert themselves and take control of where they are headed. The adage, "If you do not know where you are going, then you will probably end up lost," certainly rings true.

I will assume that if you are reading this book, it is because you are either reluctant to ride or have been unable to ride your horse, and this is because, on some level, you have fear. Call it stress or consternation or anxiety, or any other name you choose, but what it comes down to, in the end, can accurately be labeled as fear. This is nothing to be ashamed of. After all, the truth is, equestrian activities can be dangerous. People get stepped on, knocked down, kicked, bitten, and dumped off when riding. Horses are a whole lot bigger than us, and although generally, the animals are not mean by nature, they are living, breathing entities with moods and minds of their own. Some will test you and try to see what they can get away with; others are somewhat guarded and easily frightened by a myriad of things they perceive as possibly dangerous threats. Things can happen in a hurry, and if you are unlucky enough to be in the way when they do, then too bad for you because it is very likely that you will get hurt.

Experienced horsemen and women know their horses and are vigilant about picking up on things that might spook the animals. This can often be the difference between a close call and an unfortunate incident. The bottom line is, however careful you might be, anyone who spends their time in the company of horses can and will get banged up a bit here and there. That is the deal, and eventually, chances are good that it is just bound to happen at some point. When my youngest daughter fell in love with horses and started hanging around the barns, I told her that if she wanted to play with horses, it was not a matter of if, but more a matter of when, and just figure that it really is just a matter of time before something happens that will cause you to get injured. I tried to school her so that she might be able to be vigilant and as careful as she possibly could to not unnecessarily put herself in a dangerous position. The best any of us can do is to be mindful of being as safe as possible; hopefully, that may allow us to mitigate how often and badly we might get injured. Now I am probably overstating the risk we take when we decide to become horse people. Thankfully, the vast majority of the horses I have crossed paths with over the almost sixty years that I have been at it are very kind. They mean us no harm, but they can panic. The young ones don't know any better, and outside of a broken wrist and more than a few broken toes, most of my injuries were no more than a scrape or a bruise, but I have just been lucky so far and am hopeful that my lucky streak will hold up. All of that said, I do not want to sugar-coat reality.

    I am saying all of this not to frighten anyone, but I do want to be honest, and this is really how I see it. That just seems to be the way it is. People can and do get hurt, and there is always going to be some level of risk involved. Now the same can be said for most of life. Living life has its risks. It is just that living your life around horses adds a few more. Growing up, the woman who lived next door was a little odd. She must have been extremely worried because I rarely saw either of her daughters come outside to play with the rest of the neighborhood kids, definitely less than ten times a year. Honestly, I cannot remember ever going into their house, so I could not say if the walls were padded. I felt kind of sorry for those girls and know they missed out on a lot of fun, but then again, they also never needed to be taken to the emergency ward of the local hospital, at least as far as I know. Everyone has choices about how they want to live their lives and how they want to spend their time. Those who decide to spend that time in the company of horses must be willing to accept that some degree of additional risk is involved. Those who choose not to will miss out on the joy that comes with spending their time with horses. I am not here to sugar-coat the truth and that there is some inherent risk one must accept. In my state, due to liability concerns, most barn owners post a sign warning that equestrian activities can be dangerous and that if you want to come onto the property, you must take responsibility for yourself.

That said, for the most part, horses are very kind beasts and not out to hurt anyone, but they sometimes do play rough. The bottom line is that whether or not you spend part of your life around horses is totally up to you. Decide whether it is worth it to accept the reality that you might get hurt at some point. If being around horses makes you feel too afraid to continue, it is probably a good idea to find something else to do with your time. If you ultimately decide that what draws you to being around horses is just too strong to resist, then keep reading. Hopefully, I can share some things that you will find useful as you make an informed decision and in navigating your path going forward.

Then ask yourself, what is really going on here? The truth is that being around the barn is probably a lot less dangerous than driving to the barn. What is happening is that most of the fear a person experiences happens because they are scaring themselves with their thoughts. Perhaps, they remember when they fell off their mount, and the thought it could happen again frightens them more than anything. Other times it is just the thoughts that they are dwelling on about what could possibly happen that worries them the most. And the good news is that this is not a difficult fix. We can control our thoughts, and it can be just a matter of thinking about more useful things. Some might argue that they cannot stop thinking about things that frighten them. This is not true. It may be that they have not yet learned how to train their mind and how to choose which thoughts they decide to focus their attention on. This can be learned and learned rather easily.

There are many ways to take control of one's thoughts. The first thing we need to do is become aware of those thoughts that are not helpful. It will be easier to stop those pesky negative thoughts if we wear a rubber band around our wrist and snap it whenever we have an unproductive one. Certainly, random thoughts will pop up in our heads. Perhaps from something we see or hear or at other times, a thought may simply spontaneously arise. And I totally agree that there is no way to control that from happening occasionally, but we can decide to change what we think about. It is up to us to allow our minds to wander and imagine horrible things happening or dismiss those thoughts and put our attention elsewhere. It might not happen right away, but we can train our minds, and the more we take control, the easier it becomes. When we catch ourselves thinking unhelpful things, we can imagine hitting the delete button on a keyboard and picture in big, bold black letters DELETE. This works well for many people. The key is to have an image or a memory to fill the empty space right away. It could be a picture of a person or animal or a place we remember. Something that evokes a warm feeling or brings a smile to our face. It is a good idea to think of these scenes ahead of time so that when needed, we can bring the image to the forefront of our minds. If a person is not visually oriented, they could use a song that stirs up good feelings or simply recall a feeling or sensation. The secret is to catch ourselves when we think unhelpful thoughts and interrupt the pattern. Preferably we catch ourselves sooner rather than later, but it works no matter how long the thought has been looping in our mind.

Another very effective way to interrupt the thought loop is to use Emotional Freedom Technique (EFT). This involves tapping on specific acupressure points and finishing by firing off an anchor to close off the process. There are various ways to do this, and I will share the method I use. Tap with two fingers hard enough to hear a little thud but not so hard that it hurts. The points I use are as follows:

- between the eyes (some call this area the "third eye")
- alongside the outside of the eye (temple area)
- on the cheekbone below the eye
- at one inch on either or both sides of the collarbone (I usually use three or four fingers and tap all around this area)
- then fire off an anchor that has been previously installed, which I will describe how to do in a moment

Before I do that, I want to add a few important details.

Before you begin to tap, it is helpful to weigh in on how these thoughts you have been thinking are making you feel at that moment. Rate the feeling, whether it be anxiety, anger, stress, or whatever other word you use to label the feeling on a scale of one (very weak) to ten (very strong). This way, you can gauge where you start and compare it to where you are when you finish. It is essential to recognize and acknowledge how strong the feelings are at the start and compare them to where they are when you finish. The other thing you want to do as you are tapping is to give yourself suggestions such as "Let it go," "It is not helpful to hold on to," "Release the feeling . . . and watch it disappear," and any other things of that nature that will help you let go of the unhelpful thoughts and corresponding feelings attached to those thoughts. Run through that tapping pattern as you give yourself suggestions to let go of the thoughts. Then top it off by firing an anchor.

An anchor is a touch, a picture, a smell, or a sound that you associate with a feeling or a state. Perhaps you've heard of Ivan Pavlov, a scientist who ran an experiment feeding dogs. Before he would feed them, he would ring a bell just before feeding the dogs, and after a short while, the dogs began to associate the sound of the bell with being fed. As soon as the bell was rung, the dogs would get excited and start to salivate and drool. These associations are formed naturally and are used in advertising and marketing. A song you hear may bring on pleasant memories and nostalgic feelings. The tone of your spouse's voice may be enough to make you feel uneasy and give you the sense that trouble is coming. The aroma of apple pie reminds you of grandma. You begin to experience feelings of warmth. These are naturally forming anchors.

The way to set an anchor is to have the person remember a memory as they touch a spot and then build up and amplify the feeling to a peak level and then let it go. Distract them and then do it again a few more times until just the touch will evoke the feeling you want them to experience. The way I help them set this anchor is to have them recall, say, a peaceful, pleasant memory. I will have them press their thumb on the inside of their wrist and wrap the other fingers around it. As they do this, I will ask them to see what they were looking at, hear the sounds they heard, feel what they were feeling, or smell or taste what they had been experiencing. In other words, help them to re-live the experience and build it up and then take a deep breath and, on the exhale, say to themselves, "peace." After building up the feeling that the memory evokes, have them let go of their wrist and forget the memory by distracting them with an unrelated question about something entirely different. Then I will repeat the process a couple more times to condition the association, and the anchor will be set. All of this is a lot to process just by reading about it. This works well, and to fully grasp it, I encourage you to visit my website at www.equestrianhypnocoach.com where you will be able to watch a video that will give more clarity and a better understanding of how to do the process.

Once you have set the anchor, anytime you catch yourself thinking unhelpful or upsetting thoughts, you simply check in and see where you are on a one-to-ten scale.

Begin tapping on the aforementioned points while giving yourself suggestions to let go and relax. Finish by firing the anchor, pressing thumb on the inside of the wrist and wrapping your hand around it, taking a deep breath, and saying "peace," allowing that to settle for a moment. Then, check in on a scale of one to ten to see where you are. If you are not down to a one or a zero, repeat the process until you are at a one or a zero. The only caveat I have is to tell you that this process will only work if you actually do it! And the more often you do it, the better it works until you get to the point where you no longer need to do it much at all because new habits are formed. Instead of thinking thoughts that frighten you and allowing those thoughts to recycle over and over in your head, getting you more and more anxious and upset, you will eventually no longer entertain them at all. And it can be just that easy to re-program and re-wire your brain.

It used to be believed that when we are young, it is easy to change how our brain functions, and the brain can be rerouted, but once we mature and the older we get, the less likely that is to happen. When we age, the way we think becomes locked in, and we can no longer make changes. After all, you can't teach an old dog new tricks, right? Well, the truth is that neuroscientists have discovered that it is not true. The fact is that the human brain remains malleable throughout a person's lifetime. Some describe the brain as being plastic; the technical term for this is neuroplasticity. The only thing that may make it seem as though an older person cannot change the way they think is simply the belief that you are set in your ways.

CHAPTER 3

Thoughts and Thinking

I was first introduced to The Three Principals a couple of years ago while being coached by a very influential mentor, Mr. James Tripp. Also known as Inside-Out Thinking or Psychology of Mind, it was discovered and developed by a man named Sydney Banks, who had no formal schooling beyond the ninth grade without any training or credentials in the field of psychology. Sydney, a welder by trade, lived in Scotland and was an ordinary man with an experience in 1971 that profoundly affected him and set him on the path in search of enlightenment. The story goes that Mr. Banks had been going to a group marriage counseling session and went outside during a break to smoke. It was there when he commented to one of the psychologists out there that he was feeling very stressed out. The psychologist told Sydney that he was not that stressed out but rather the case that he just "thought" he was stressed out. As he began to ponder this offhand comment, Mr. Banks began to understand the importance behind what he had just heard and the realization of just how true this statement was. As he delved even deeper into the idea, he came to understand that just about everything a person experiences in life does not come from external circumstances, that it is not what happens to them or outside of them, but rather all of a person's experiences in life are due to their thoughts about what happens outside of them. Now on the surface, many people might readily agree with this and see it as a very simplistic and logical assumption. It requires one to take a deep look to fully comprehend the power that comes from understanding the magnitude of this idea and fully appreciate just how profound this concept can be when you follow it further. It can be a game changer once it sinks in on a deeper level. Everything we do and believe starts with and is in reaction to our thoughts. We can begin to see that we have a lot more control over what and how we think than we may have ever realized before. This realization can open us up to infinite possibilities and entertain the ideas of what is possible for us to achieve. For those interested in taking a deeper look, there are a lot of good books out there. What I am offering here is merely a cursory look at all that was uncovered by the work of Sydney Banks.

The Three Principals are *Mind* (and more specifically, the connection between your mind and what some might call the Universal Mind or Universal Wisdom), *Consciousness* (that which you are aware of or the sense that you make out of what you are thinking about), and *Thought*. Many people tend to confuse their thoughts with facts. This happens to all of us from time to time. Whenever a person accepts a thought as the truth, they automatically shut down any further examination, and further inquiry stops as one simply begins accepting from then on that thought as being a fact. After one thinks the same thought repeatedly for long enough, it becomes a belief. Sometimes these beliefs limit us, and because we accept them as being true, we cease ever to question their validity any further. James Tripp refers to these limiting beliefs as "cherished truths," which is a fairly accurate portrayal of what is happening here. People hold out their limiting beliefs as truths because fact is truth (because they really do seem to be true), and so they cling to and cherish them and never even begin to question their veracity. There is also no consideration over whether or not said belief serves them. It is simply accepted that this is how things are, and behaviors are adjusted accordingly. We relinquish the idea that we can exert any control over them.

One good way to challenge these beliefs is to ask the following questions, which come from *The Work* by Byron Katie. Katie's work can be examined more closely by reading one of the many books she has put out about how she goes about affecting change. It has helped many people re-examine and see their beliefs in a whole new light. First, ask yourself, "Is this statement, this belief true?" If you answer yes and continue to see it as being true, then ask yourself to reconsider the question, "Are you absolutely certain that this is indeed true?" Next, ask, "So how does believing this thought make me feel?" This question dissuades you from arguing over what is or is not true and instead focuses your attention on what is useful. One can argue all day about the question of what is or is not true, but that may not be the best question to ask. The much better question to ask is whether something is useful or not. Look instead and consider whether that thought is serving me or stopping me. Is it taking me further toward or farther away from becoming the person I want to become? This is the much more important question to put your attention towards. Your mind and the thoughts you entertain can be your most powerful asset. They can help put you on the path toward becoming an unstoppable force in the world. Unfortunately, for some people, their minds and the thoughts they choose to believe can also be the very thing that stops them in their tracks.

The human mind can accurately be said to be the world's most powerful computer that enables us to do some very complex maneuvers. Couple that with an autonomous nature, and by that, I mean our ability to decide what we want and choose to do with it, which increases our personal power that much more. We are the only creatures on earth with the cognitive abilities to think about and decide what we want to think about. No other mammal in the animal kingdom has the capacity to travel through the world like this. We take in data using our five senses: visual, auditory, kinesthetic, gustatory, and olfactory—what we see, hear, feel, taste, and smell. Also, there is no denying the existence of a sixth sense in our possession (this gets us back to the connection between our mind and Universal Wisdom). We come into this world in possession of the most powerful computer known to be in existence but without the advantages of having been given any owner's manual telling us exactly how to use these powers we have. So far as our mind and how it operates goes, the two most powerful of these senses come from the pictures we make in our heads, the words we tell ourselves, and the words we hear. We have a lot of room to decide how to best use these two modalities, visual and auditory, in the most effective way possible. In the following chapters, we will explore further how we might best be able to do this to further enhance and optimize our capabilities. Visualization and self-talk are so important that they deserve separate chapters dealing with each. And so, why do I mention this, and why is it important for those who seek to overcome their fears which might have led them to hesitate or even develop an aversion, to continue engaging in what is perhaps one of their greatest joys in life, riding their horse? And my answer to that question is the same whether this behavior has come from an unfortunate incident, like when they once fell off their mount and were injured, or whether it originates from an imagined fear of what could happen, or maybe the discomfort that comes from being judged too harshly by others for any mistakes they might make while riding.

One very useful follow-up question to ask yourself is this: Do I believe that I can make this happen? If your answer to this question is "No, do not believe I can do this," then we need to talk. To change, people must believe that it is possible. If they can see that other people who came before them could do it, there is proof that it is possible. Then they must come to see that it is also possible for them and that they can make the same change. This comes down to believing in their own personal power. Most people have no clue just how powerful they actually are. There is a story about a man struggling financially in his business and playing scared, always focusing on the possibility that things could go wrong, and if they did, his whole business would come crashing down, and he could be left in ruin. He became stuck, frozen, and afraid to make any move for fear of the consequences. He was afraid to hire more people; he was afraid to invest in more inventory. And because of the inability to do these things when things picked up and got busier, his company was unable to meet the needs of his customers, and they looked elsewhere to get their needs met. Everything he did and did not do seemed to work against the success of his business. He sat on a park bench in utter despair, contemplating his dilemma. Then a well-dressed gentleman sat beside him and, seeing this man was in a bad way, asked him what was wrong. The struggling businessman opened up to the stranger and began telling the other man about his problems. The more he shared his tales of woe, the better he began to feel. When he was finished unloading his burdens, he felt lighter and better.

As they spoke further, he found out that this well-dressed fellow was very successful himself, and one of the things he did that made him wealthy was invest in small businesses, and when they made a profit, he shared in their fortune. He offered to help the struggling business owner but was turned down because he feared he would be unable to pay back the debt. Eventually, they came to an agreement that went like this: The wealthy man would write the business owner a check for a substantial sum of money. If things got bad enough, the business owner would have the option to roll the dice and cash the check, and they agreed on terms regarding the investor's share in the profits that ensued. They hammered out the details, and after coming to terms, both could agree on they wrote them down and signed their names to it, and they agreed to meet again one year later. The well-dressed man pointed to a nearby building where he said his office was located and said he could be found there. The business owner pointed to the other end of the park and explained how all he had to do was ask for him by name so his staff would see they were connected. After they shook hands, they each went their way. As fate would have it, things gradually improved in the man's business, and although he was comforted by having the option available, he never found the need to cash the man's check. After a year had passed, he went in search of the business investor and walked past the park bench and into the building where the man's office was located. There he was surprised to find that there were no offices and only a welcoming window which he approached in search of information on how to find his benefactor. When he asked for him by name, the receptionist seemed puzzled by his inquiry. It was after he described the man's attire that the lady at the desk smiled and informed him that the place he entered was a mental institution and the man he described was a patient there who was delusional and thought he was a wealthy angel investor and told that the check he carried in his wallet was worthless and had no value. The business owner was both shocked at hearing this news and frightened because all along, he had been making bold moves in his business fortified by his ace in the hole, which was useless. Any of those bold moves could have burnt him, destroyed his business, and left him bankrupt and destitute. But because he believed he had an option at any time to cash the check in his pocket, his outlook and mindset were completely changed. This was the underlying reason he could overcome his business challenges. As so often is the case, when our mindset changes, everything else does as well.

There is a way of thinking and a strategy for approaching life known as "the be-do-have model." Most people go through the world operating in a way that goes something like this: If I *do* this or that, then I can *have* such and such desired outcome, and from here, I can *be* like this. In other words, if I behave (*do*) this, then I will get (*have*) that and become (*be*) this kind of person.

The be-do-have model turns things around and tells us: If I am (*be*) like this in the world, I will *do* things that will allow me to *have* this result. So, first *become*, then *behave*, and then you will *have* the outcome you desire. It starts with being the kind of person who does things that will allow them to have these other things. The be-do-have model tells us that it all starts with who we are being and not with what we are doing. When the man in the story earlier had that worthless check in his pocket, he began to see the world in a brand-new way and then started being different. After he started being this way, he began doing things differently and got completely different results. The question becomes, who would you be without the fear that you could fail? What might you do with a million-dollar check in your pocket? Would you ever even need to cash it if you had the security of knowing that you could if you needed to? And what might be possible for you with the mindset alone?

Once upon a time, things happened in my life that set things on their head. Try as I might to get things to turn out the way I wanted them to, but I failed. I failed to exert my will and control over life, and believe me, I tried as hard as a man could possibly try. Finally, I had to give up trying to control life circumstances. I had no choice but to leave it in the hands of a power greater than me. I called this power God, and you might call it something else. Anyway, long story short, things ended up working out much better than they could have, even if I had been able to control every last tiny detail myself. They worked out better because, at that point, I was forced to let go of the illusion that I was in control over the outcome. In other words, I was not in a position to even entertain the notion that it was possible, which is why it exceeded my expectations. The thing is that ever since all of those things happened, I have come to believe that everything will work out favorably once the dust settles. Now I am not about to argue whether this is true. I know that in the end, none of us will get out of this life alive. But for me, I cannot help but believe that everything will work out for the best, and I know that this has been more true than not in my life. And so, I will pose another question for you to consider, "How much would you worry if you knew that no matter where things are at this moment, things are going to work out for the best?" And follow that with "Who would you be, without the worry?" Indeed, there is no way to ensure that everything in your life will work out exactly the way you wish or plan for. In life, there are zero guarantees as to the outcome, but what if there was a way to eliminate the worry? When circumstances change, we have no other option but to adapt and keep moving. It is not the change of circumstance as much as it is the fear and worries over things we do not control that keeps us stuck in a place that limits us. I would argue that the worry, more than anything else, is most detrimental.

    A person cannot just choose to just start believing something new right away, even if it would be useful for them to do so. To believe something new usually means they will have to stop believing something that is stopping them from accepting the new way of thinking. For this to happen, they usually want to see some evidence. This is both reasonable and understandable. Now I am not about to suggest that you abandon your beliefs. For starters, I do not think it is possible and do not even think it would be wise. Your beliefs have got you this far in life. Most of them are probably useful. When we are young children, it is easy for us to pretend, and as we grow and we learn more and more, we start accepting ideas that, over time, make it harder to pretend or even imagine things differently. This is sad because imagination is such a tremendously powerful ability. The funny thing is that we often imagine what would happen if things went bad, and these types of thoughts stop us from doing things that could end up being helpful for us. What if we were able to suspend our disbelief in order to open ourselves up to what just might be possible?

This is probably a good time for me to mention just how important it is to pay attention to where we are and what we are thinking. Often the first thing people notice is the feeling, the body sensation, and the thought that came before it goes unnoticed. We first must notice the thoughts that immediately precede our behaviors. Everything starts with a thought; far too often, people mistake what we think is a fact and not merely a thought. We are poor witnesses to the processes that drive our behavior. Number one, pay attention to what you are thinking and to what you are telling yourself. It has been said that a fish in a fishbowl is not likely to be aware of the water. The water is just there all the time and not being noticed. What if you were to consider that we are swimming in our thoughts all the time? It has been said typically, around 70,000 thoughts each day (though many of these are not new, a repetition of the same thought loops). Whatever that actual number of thoughts for you, let's agree that we all have a whole lot of thoughts constantly running through our minds. So first, start paying attention to what you are thinking and then notice what meaning you are making about those thoughts: I am thinking [this], and so it must mean [that]. Only by doing this are you ever going to see what you are actually doing to scare yourself. Go ahead and read that last sentence again. That is right! What is really going on here is you are thinking thoughts that are making you afraid. It is not what your horse is doing that scares you the most. It is more likely what you are thinking about and the meaning you make to those thoughts, the what-ifs!

Let's get back to motivation and allow me to pose a couple of questions you might find useful to ponder. And do not rush right through them. Hang around them a bit and notice what you think about your answers and what those thoughts mean. The first is the "big why." *Why* do you ride, and *why* do you want to continue to ride? Does it really mean that much to you, and is it worth it for you to continue to engage in the sport, or is it time to pack up you boots and britches and partake in life's more sedentary pursuits? Almost everything in life carries some risk; weighing out the risk-reward equation is a personal decision. For most people who ride a well-behaved horse, there is probably a far greater risk of being injured while driving to the barn than after you mount up. The only thing stopping you from thinking differently is the very thought that you cannot control those thoughts. You have the power to decide, and you do have the power to control your thoughts, to control your behavior, and to control your life as well as your destiny. If you want to hold onto your thoughts, that is your choice. I respect that it is your choice to make. I want you to be aware that this is what is actually going on. You are only a victim to your thoughts if the thought you are thinking is, "I have no control over my thoughts and can't help but think what I am thinking." You are bigger and more powerful than your thoughts! And if you are not yet able to fully accept and believe this, then I suggest you just for a single day, set that aside and pretend that you are bigger and act as if you are more powerful and pay attention to what happens next because it is here that you will find the evidence to support the truth behind this new way of thinking.

The real problem with thinking things that are stopping you is not that you will take action and then fail. The bigger problem is that holding on to these limiting beliefs will cause you to fail to act at all. This is at the heart of what these stories we tell ourselves about ourselves do to us. The world is filled with people who are not living the lives they were meant to live. It is filled with people who never reach their full potential, and never achieve their dreams, not because they tried and failed but because they failed to try. And it always comes down to the stories they tell themselves. Those stories sound and seem to be true. Stop making yourself afraid by thinking thoughts that make you afraid. Ultimately what stops us is not because of what has happened or might happen to us. It is almost always because of our what-if thoughts that we allow our gloom and doom projections to stop us dead in our tracks. Truth be told, yes, the worst possible scenario could happen, but the odds are the very best possible outcome is just as likely to occur.

Many times, when it comes to a Worst Possible Scenario (WPS), we stop the story right at the moment when the result seems most devastating because we stop asking the question, "Then what happens?" An example may go something like this:

"I do not want to ride right now because there are too many people milling around, and if my horse acts up and I am unable to control him, I will look like a fool. The people watching will think I am inept, then they will talk about me and laugh at me behind my back."

The story playing out in their mind stops. Let's rewind and rewrite the story:

"My horse acts up, and I am unable to control him fully, but I persevere and refuse to give up and continue to try my best to regain some semblance of control until I wear him down and he gets tired of goofing around. I can stop him. Then I patiently and slowly put him through his paces again, and this time he holds it together for a little while longer before he once again starts his antics, and we go through the cycle until I can regain control again. And what might these people think about me now, and why do I even care anyway? Why does the opinion of these people matter to me? Are they going to stop liking me? And why is that important to me? And are they going to stop being my friends? What kind of friends were they in the first place? And does this mean they will stop paying my bills so I can continue to eat and survive? Well, if they actually are footing my bills, then maybe I will not risk messing up that deal and decide not to ride today after all."

Hopefully, you get the idea I am trying to drive home here, and that is we have a lot of options regarding what story we tell ourselves, and far too often, if the one we had been telling is not doing us much good, then why not change it to a different story?

There are times when the story might be true, and if that is the case, we better look at options other than just changing the storyline. Some horses buck too hard or rear up too high or have such a "dead" and unresponsive mouth they run off on us, and we cannot stop them. Some animals are just too afraid and spooky to make a good riding horse, and some are just too mean, but this is very rare and unlikely. What do we do then? If we cannot get them re-broke and retrained or get the instructions and experience we need to ride them safely, then our best bet may be to sell them and replace them with a better horse. It is not the end of the world. It is not the first time a rider and their mount are not a good fit for each other. We cannot dismiss the possibility that it may be the case, and perhaps it is time to find a better horse for us to enjoy. However, most of the time, the biggest problem we face comes down to our thoughts, which drive our behavior and determine the experience, and sometimes just knowing this can make a difference.

Imagine we were consultants, business consultants, and we helped corporate executives, as well as business owners and operators, deal with the problems and concerns that face them. And one day into our office comes a highly successful business owner looking for our help. And we asked him what he needed, and he told us that what he needed was to become quicker because things were happening so fast in his line of work. He needed to act right in the moment in order to stay ahead of things. And he also said that he needed to become more flexible because the deal he was chasing had a lot of twists and turns and required him to change direction on a dime and go another way. And then he said the third thing he needed was to have a better strategy because it seemed like no matter what he did and which way he went, the thing he was after seemed to be able to read his mind and always seemed to be one step ahead of him and forever just out of reach. Because we needed a little more information, we asked him if we could watch him in action so we could see for ourselves in real time what was happening, and he agreed to allow us to do this. And oh yeah, I forgot to mention this business owner was actually a dog! But as I said at the start, we just imagine all of this anyway. The day comes when we get to follow him and see for ourselves what is going on here. And we watch him carefully as he tries to get ahead of things and get what he is after. And it only takes a short while before we can see exactly what he is up against. At the end of the day, he asks us what we think, and we look at each other and then turn to him and say, "Look, we talked about this a bit, and both agree that we do not think you need to become quicker, and we also do not believe being more flexible is the answer either. And we are pretty sure that a new strategy is not going to do you much good because it is very clear to us that what has been going on here all along is that you have been chasing your own tail. Now, the business owner can only respond in one of three ways to our observation. He could say, "You guys are crazy, and you are fired because I need to go somewhere else to find what I need to do." Or he could lean back in his chair, rubbing his chin, and say, "Wow! Of course! Oh my gosh! How did I not see that is what has been happening all this time? How could I have missed it? Thank you both so much for your input. It has been very valuable to me to become aware of this." Or the third response he might come up with "Oh, I see! I totally understand now. Of course, none of these things that I thought I needed would do me any good at all. And to think that I have been chasing my tail all this time. How foolish of me not to notice. And so, gentlemen, what do you think I should do now?" As I said, sometimes just knowing what is going on is enough. Then there are other times a person may say they see what is happening, but in reality, they do not. They may even agree that yes, this is what is happening, but if they cannot see for themselves what they need to do, and that is changing what they are doing, it is only because, although they may see it, they are not fully comprehending what they are seeing. A person who fully understands will never need to be told the obvious, "Stop chasing your tail!"

CHAPTER 4

Emotional Mastery

Humans are not at the mercy of our emotions. We determine our experience. Emotions play a huge part in how we react and behave, and it is useful to understand exactly what is going on so that we can take control of situations as they unfold. Although emotions and feelings are often used interchangeably, there is a difference as they are not quite one and the same thing. The interrelationship and chain of reaction between the two happen in a split second, so it can be difficult to notice the distinctions between them. Emotions are stimulated by an outside stimulus, what we see, hear, feel, taste, or smell inside our physical brain. Immediately after an emotion is triggered, you will get a feeling, which is your conscious perception of that emotion. If we are ever to develop a successful strategy to gain some degree of control over our emotions, we first need to get clear about what is happening inside our minds and bodies. Then we must be aware enough to recognize it all happening inside us. It starts with an understanding of the processes and then a recognition in the moments that things are unfolding. The importance of this will become clearer as we move through this chapter. Often, when a person is ignorant of what is taking place or oblivious to the processes going on inside of themselves and in such instances, things will quickly escalate and spiral out of their control. If one is going to be able to take charge of these processes, it is much easier and more likely to take control early on than after the feelings escalate.

    Let me start by saying that emotions are neither good nor bad. Just as the function of a firearm is neutral in terms of the consequence, the same can be said for emotions. In the hands of "a good guy," a gun can protect us and those we care for from present danger. If that same weapon is being wielded by a person whose intent is to rob us or do us harm, it can cause significant damage. An emotion is merely a signal. Just like a light on the dashboard of a car, it alerts us that something is going on that needs our attention. We often think of some emotions as being inherently bad or in a negative light, while others are seen as being positive. Take anger as an example. Some may think that it is a bad thing to get angry. We feel bad and tend to act impulsively without giving time for thoughtful reflection; in many circumstances, this argument can hold merit. But what if an aggressive person is trying to detrimentally subject their will upon us or take advantage of us somehow? Then it is only because as we go through the experience, anger is triggered, and we might assert ourselves and stand our ground and not allow ourselves to be victimized in the situation. Or suppose we begin to feel an emotion that we might label as boredom, frustration, or dissatisfaction. Now the feelings we get may seem unpleasant, and because of this, we might be inclined to take some action to rectify the situation. The feelings associated with being bored caused us to act, which now makes us feel satisfied. The initial sensations may not have been pleasurable, but the action that followed may have served us beneficially, so would you then judge those feelings as good or bad? Hopefully, you can see my point that the boredom was neither good nor bad but merely a signal that we should put our attention here so that we can then decide to allow those feelings to continue or take some kind of action to change the situation.

Let's explore this a bit further and shine a light on what is happening here. Something happens and we experience it through one or more of our five senses or even through our sixth sense, which we can call our intuition for the purposes of this discussion. And whatever that initial stimulus happens to be, it causes an emotional reaction to occur inside our brain. This, in turn, instantly causes a glandular release of a neurochemical to be released into our body, causing a physical sensation. Now in the case of joy, that chemical may feel wonderful, or in the case of fear, that chemical that is released may be unpleasant. Now, we can label these embodied sensations as being pleasant or not, hence good or bad, or experienced positively or negatively. We can certainly label the feeling as being one we either like or a sensation we do not like to feel. But the emotion behind that feeling is neither positive nor negative. This is because it is purely a neutral signal, the sole purpose being that it lights up and alerts us to put our attention here, so we can then decide, "I want it to stop," or "I want more of this feeling I like." When an emotion is triggered, the chemical release happens instantly and lasts for less than sixty-to-ninety seconds, followed by a refractory period that may last longer. After that, the physical sensation will dissipate, and by ninety seconds, all sensation will completely disappear. If you read that again, I am saying that within sixty to ninety seconds, the entire emotional spike process will be completed. The anger, the fear, the sadness, and the joy will run full cycle in a minute and a half at the most! The only way these feelings can continue is if you cause them to go beyond that time span by thinking thoughts that re-ignite the emotion and consequential feelings that follow.

The other thing to mention here is that there is always a level of intensity that goes from weak and barely perceptual all the way up to strong or even overwhelming. Initially, depending upon the intensity of the reaction to whatever triggers the emotion is certainly a factor but not one that we can exert all that much control over. If a person had an experience when a Doberman pinscher dog had attacked them in the past, say as a child, when they walk down an alley and see a loose Doberman roaming the streets, it is a natural human response for an intense level of fear to show up. Because they remember being severely bitten by that breed of dog, they have no choice but to respond the way they do. This is uncontrollable, and other than doing everything humanly possible to avoid being in that situation in the first place, there is no point spending a lot of energy on something out of their control anyway. It is not the initial level of intensity that is the most impactful of all components, but the response they have to that initial emotional trigger that makes more of a difference.

Let me explain the way this entire process unfolds. There is an event that takes place that creates an emotional response. Typically, many people are unaware of any of the content we have covered here; in that case, they are simply unaware. It does not matter whether they do not understand what is happening inside of them or do not recognize at that moment this is what is happening inside of them. They start unaware, and from here, perhaps some confusion sets in. "Why am I feeling this way? I do not like this feeling and do not know how to make it stop." Then, frustration may soon follow. "I feel like I am going out of control don't know if I am even ready for this." After that, maybe even anger will surface. "I can't believe this is happening again, and I just give up and want to get out of here."

The uneasy feelings may creep in when they see their horse standing there, tacked up next to the mounting block. As they notice some of their barn mates milling around the riding area, their tensions rise, and they start feeling even worse. They begin to think that they will be judged unkindly, and their tension increases even more. All the while, they do not understand where these feelings are coming from in the first place. Then they start to think about all of the what-ifs that could possibly happen, all the things that could go wrong, and now real fear starts to set in—disgusted with themselves and the whole situation. There comes the point where they have no choice but to quickly find some excuse to go back to the barn because today is not a good day to ride. All of this takes place so fast that they are unprepared or do not know how else to deal with it all. This fear emotion had begun to spiral out of control so fast it could make your head spin. Maybe they had a bad experience falling off their mount, or the horse got out of their control, and they wildly ran back to the barn after a ride on the trails, leaving them no more than a helpless passenger praying that the ride will end with them left unharmed. Certainly, in one of these scenarios, the rider could possibly explain the why behind their experience. Honestly, it does not matter all that much whether they start out merely slightly uncomfortable or much closer to panic. And truthfully, whether they have a legitimate reason or it is only a matter of thoughts gone wild does not make all that much difference either because the mind reacts just as strongly to real life or imagined danger. The only difference here is that if it is, in fact, a "real" danger because if your mount is not well trained enough for you to control them or your skills as a rider are not strong enough to control your horse, the only sensible recourse may be to sell that particular horse and find one that is more suitable to fit your level of ability as an equestrian. Although that may be a topic of conversation well worth considering, what we are talking about here is your ability to control your emotional response. The point I am trying to make here is that a negative emotional spiral often can and will happen very quickly. This is why I am emphasizing the importance of being aware and vigilant because once you get caught in a downward spiral, it becomes more difficult to turn things around.

This begets the question of what one can do to master or even begin to take control of their emotions. To break it down, assuming you have a good grasp on what is happening, and if you are following me this far, we can pretty safely assume that, at this point, you now have a handle on the understanding part. From here, you want to label the emotion as it comes up. By naming it, as you are identifying it, you are giving it a handle easier to deal with. Then, think back carefully, paying attention to a specific time in the past when you did have an unwanted emotion crop up. Perhaps the last time, or the last memorable time this has happened to you. You may have to slow down the thought process, carefully taking the memory bit by bit to see if you can catch the exact moment or slightly before the moment you first began to notice the associated feeling. We are looking for the trigger here. This is usually something you heard or saw. Something someone said or something you said to yourself. Or perhaps something you saw, maybe a look on someone's face, or something that you pictured in your mind. This could, of course, stem from a memory of a bad experience or maybe you saw something happen to another rider that you might fear could happen to you. When you realize what triggered the emotion, write it down and chronicle it. According to noted University of Texas researcher James Pennebaker, writing it down does a couple of things. For starters, it engages different areas of the brain, which helps you to acknowledge and remember the trigger. It can also help you better understand what is important to you. After writing it down on paper, you want to re-frame the underlying meaning. For instance, if you notice a crowd of people watching, instead of thinking, "Oh no, everyone will be watching me," which will only cause an increase of pressure on you, make a conscious decision to say something like "It is a good thing that most people are so self-absorbed because they will likely not have the bandwidth to be paying any attention to me as I ride." You want to identify, label, then write down the trigger and explore the meaning you are making, which causes the upset within you. Then play around trying on different meanings behind the trigger until you find some that are plausible enough to negate the uncomfortable feelings. You want to do this for any and all specific triggers you can recall. On top of this, you want to be alert to any time in the future that you experience uncomfortable feelings. After you are done riding, go through the same process, identify the emotion, name it, and re-frame it, putting pen to paper to help integrate all of it into your being. You may even want to review what you chronicle so that when a similar situation arises, you are well prepared to respond more favorably. Once you condition it, it will establish new neural pathways in your brain. You will be rewiring your brain to begin to respond automatically in different and more useful ways. We shall take a deeper look at this in a following chapter. Keep in mind an emotion can be spiked from anything at all. It does not have to have anything to do with riding or horses for it to affect your response. If, for instance, the owner of the barn was to say something unjust or unkind to you shortly before you mount up, it could make you angry and, in turn, affect your ride. There is always an emotional refractory period that may last well beyond the emotional reactive response time. Suppose someone cuts you off in traffic and gets in front of you, and shortly after that, they jam on their brakes and then wait to turn off the road, and now here you are, stuck waiting behind them. This angers you, and a short while later, you find yourself irritated by another motorist who does less to annoy you. But because your anger had already been set off by the actions of the first inconsiderate driver, and that incident was still fresh on your mind, your patience with the second driver had worn thin, and you reacted even more intensely than you might have otherwise behaved. If your anger worsens, we could say you are in an angry mood. Again, moods tend to escalate, which gives credence to the idea that all of this becomes much easier to control if you catch it early in the progression cycle.

Another idea that I modified after reading John Haime's wonderful book for equestrians in need of more confidence called *Ride Big* is what he calls the Ten Second Rule. Because we already know that the emotional spike that comes from the release of neurochemicals that give us those unwanted and uncomfortable sensations will only last for a very short time. As soon as we notice the whole emotional spike process being set in motion, we pause and take a slow, deep belly breath, a pattern interrupt that will inject a para-sympathetic relaxation response into the mix. All the while, we consider what exact kind of outcome we are looking for. Then we change the channel and replace that thought with something entirely different. The brain will automatically fill in the space left open when we remove a thought, so why not have a thought already set up in advance to fill the space? I had a particularly happy memory of my grandchildren waiting in my back pocket, which never failed to bring a smile to my face. You could have a fond memory of a vacation moment or a beloved pet, or you be prepared to instantly recall something or someone that you found really funny works exceedingly well (humor is always a very powerful antidote). I would use this as a go-to strategy that I used over again to prevent myself from dropping into a dark rabbit hole that had the potential to ruin my mood or even my entire day.

 The last thing I will discuss here in this chapter on controlling and eventually mastering your emotions is the value of engaging in a gratitude practice. I will make an exception to my earlier statement about all emotions being neither good nor bad and my suggestion that we should consider them all to be neutral. I am not sure whether gratitude could or should be considered an emotion, but one thing I am certain of is that there is absolutely nothing neutral around the idea of being grateful and the feelings that come from it. Gratitude is nothing short of transformational. I cannot think of a single reason not to put our attention on things that cause us to be grateful daily. There are many ways to do this, and I will share the one I use most often. When going to bed and/or upon awakening, go through the alphabet picking out things to be grateful for. You need not hit every letter, and for me, I find it better to allow a couple of people or places or things to be grateful for on each letter.

    I will take my time in order to fully appreciate whoever or whatever my attention is focused on, when I land on the one (usually, this is a person that I significantly care about or love) that greatly moves me at that moment and then think about that particular person at different times throughout the day. Luckily for me, I have quite a few people who fit in that category, so it is always someone new. Doing this practice in advance not only starts you up on the right note but also makes it very easy to remember at that moment when your buttons might have been pushed to bring that special person to mind, think about why you are grateful that they are or at some point had been in your life. This is a fail-safe way to change the game, shrug off any unwanted reaction or behavior, and replace it with something better. Now I have not been able to do this all of the time or even on some days most of the time. But I have been able to do it some of the time. The more often you remember to focus on people and things in your life to be grateful for, the easier it is to remember to do it when it would be useful. While going through Mental Toughness Training and learning strategies and techniques while working with athletes, one of the sayings we learned and used was, "Winners win in advance." For some reason, this adage comes to mind, as does the idea that this sentiment extends far beyond just the world of sports.

CHAPTER 5

Seeing and Hearing

The primary modalities through which we take information into our psyche are by what we see with our eyes or picture in our mind (visualization) and hear with our ears or by the things we say to ourselves (affirmations). It is important that we monitor and choose to see and hear things that align with what we want out of life. Out of all the thoughts we have in a day, most of them will be the same thoughts we repeat in our heads, and for most people, most of these thoughts will be negative. This negativity bias can be explained as being part of an instinctual survival mechanism that keeps us cautious and safe from engaging in reckless behaviors. This may or may not be true, but what is certain is that if we listen to all of these negative thoughts, we will be stifled and limited in terms of what we might otherwise be able to achieve. It is easy to see that if we were to put our attention on the more positive thoughts, we would have a much better chance of optimizing our performance, eliminating habits that do not serve us, and achieving goals that would not be possible to fulfill if we allowed ourselves to be constantly beaten down and defeated by our own negative thoughts.

Many people "need to see it to believe it." At the same time, other people might suspect that when a person strongly believes it, it becomes very likely that they will see it. And no rule in the Universe precludes both beliefs from being true. It appears it matters little whether these are the things we see with our own eyes or are simply imagined in our thoughts. Many studies have been done over the years that show whether an athlete physically practices their skill sets or instead spends that same amount of time vividly imagining practicing those same skills inside their mind. The results match up very closely—in one experiment where a Division 1 college basketball team was divided into players that spent 30 minutes each day practicing free throws from the foul line ended up with a lower free throw percentage than the group that spent thirty minutes engaged in a visualization exercise. Perhaps it was because, in real-world practice, those players missed some of their shots while the other group of players was told to imagine sinking every shot perfectly without fail. Similar experiments have been done over a variety of different sports, and all the results have supported the idea that it makes little difference whether the results are real or imagined. What we believe plays a huge role in determining actual real-world results. It becomes a question of whether it is wise for us to take steps to ensure that those beliefs we hold lead us towards positive outcomes or whether we might leave it all to chance and be at the mercy of our previously mentioned bias towards negative thinking.

In the case of someone afraid or a little hesitant to ride their horse, it becomes clear that they are much better off remembering all the times they had enjoyed riding without any incident. They are better at allowing themselves to recall all the hours they spent enjoying being on horseback, whether in a ring or walking down a bridal path, cantering alongside the ocean, or in a full-out gallop across a meadow. And instead of dwelling on times when they rode a horse that spooked from a paper blowing across the trail or an incident when they fell off and hit the dirt, take just a moment to think about what they learned from these experiences. Realize that this is all part of being around horses. Those kinds of things are just a part of becoming a more experienced and seasoned horseman or woman and are useful in developing into a more proactive rather than reactive equestrian. And wouldn't it be far more useful to imagine future rides being fun and exciting rather than making yourself afraid by picturing things going the other way? Instead of wasting time thinking about the "what-ifs" that will likely never happen anyway and only make us uneasy and anxious, isn't it more useful and practical to turn them into "even ifs"? So often, people fixate their thinking on things that might go wrong and fail to realize that it is just as likely that instead of the worst possible scenario, you have the same odds that things could unfold in the very best way possible. It is a choice whether to put on our rose-colored glasses and see things through the lens of wonderful possibilities or reach for the "doom and gloom" glasses and picture things going wrong. Wearing the "doom and gloom" glasses does not keep you any safer, and wearing the rose-colored glasses makes life so much more fun! Optimistic thinking is a choice, and it is the only choice that makes sense.

It is very useful to take a bit of time out to visualize your day unfolding in a way that leads to amazing, positive outcomes, and this goes far beyond your time spent around the barn and into every facet of your life. Some people believe that the Law of Attraction is very real. In short, the positive energy you put into the world will come back to you and help make you more successful and more likely to experience more positive things happening in your life. I suspect that this may be truer than not. I certainly think there is credence to the idea that there is such a thing as a self-fulfilling prophesy. This all comes down to intention and expectancy. From where I am sitting, it must be far better to intend and expect to be a winner in life than expect to be a loser. What a sad thought to think that there are people who travel through this world, always expecting to lose and always expecting to come up on the short end of things. Your mind is, without question, your most powerful asset, but how on earth could it help you succeed with a strategy like that?

In the same way, it is up to you to determine what things you want to picture in your mind. It is critically important that you hear yourself saying things that support you, things that empower you, and things that can make you unstoppable. This is an absolute game-changer in terms of the results that you will experience in your life. Like most people, I spent a large part of my life ignoring all the little things that I did well, focusing instead on those situations where I had come up short, thinking I could have done better. It was not that I had a conscious strategy to put more attention on my failures and less on my wins, but that was, in fact, how I tended to operate. Looking back, I believe I rolled this way thinking if I paid attention to those things I got wrong, I would be less likely to repeat my same mistakes over again. I have come to understand the twisted logic did nothing to serve my interests. I now try to celebrate all of my victories, even those that in the past I would have glossed over, thinking, "Of course, I did that right. That is what I am supposed to do, and I certainly deserve no applause for doing what was the right thing to do." I was wrong in thinking this way. It is important to recognize when I get things right, even the little things. If my grandchild did something well, I would acknowledge it and compliment them. I would do that to reinforce good behavior. Why would I not be as kind to myself? The way I used to behave only caused me to keep my focus on my shortcomings. How could this help my confidence, self-esteem, and sense of self-worth? There is no upside to talking to myself this way. Never underestimate the power that comes with feeling good about yourself.

I realize that, for the most part, people are unaware that, for much of the time, people pass through life in a trance state. This is just how we are wired as humans, and that is just how it is. I will delve into this further in this book, but for now, trust me when I tell you that we must be conscious (aware) when we are first learning to do something new. When we learn to drive, we must always be aware and pay attention to how hard we press on the gas or the brake and how much we turn the steering wheel. Once a person learns how to drive, the actions required become less conscious and eventually automatic. After a few years of experience under their belts, most people can drive down the road singing along with the song on the radio, tapping their hand on the steering wheel in tune with the beat, and thinking about a million things other than driving. We learn how to do something by consciously paying attention, and over time we learn to drive automatically, unconsciously, which is to say, in a trance. This is how we are wired, and most of our time is spent in one trance or another. Hypnosis is everywhere, and the greatest hypnotist you will ever listen to is YOU! This is true because, for one, you believe the suggestions you tell yourself, and two, you tend to repeatedly think them until they sink into the deeper parts of your brain. You give yourself suggestions all the time. All day long, you tell yourself things you accept as being true. Things that, as you repeat and over time, become your beliefs. Your beliefs about yourself. I cannot stress enough just how important it is for you to pay attention to these things—to monitor these things, examine these things, you say and hear, and question them to see if they really are true. And whether you continue to see them as being true, what is an even more important question to ask is whether or not they are useful. Whether or not that thought you are hearing yourself say is taking you closer to becoming the person you aspire to become or whether that thing you are saying and hearing is taking you further away from the person you want to be. I cannot emphasize enough how important this is, as what you say to yourself in private will have a significant impact on who you are now and who you will become in the future. It will determine what you think you can or cannot do. It will determine how you behave and what kind of a life you will have.

    Most people pay very little attention to the specific words that they use. Pay careful attention to each and every word you say to yourself because sometimes you can say things using different but similar words, and so on the surface, you will seem to be saying exactly the same thing, but you are not! You see, words not only convey information. Words are loaded; by that,

I mean they carry connotations that elicit very specific feelings, and sometimes each one holds a very different emotional charge. And this is not always constant. In other words, a word that has an emotional impact on me might not have the same effect on you. For now, suffice to say that the charge a word holds may vary from person to person and largely is determined by the meaning that a particular person is making when they hear the word. Often this can be contextual and may depend on the state the listener happens to be in when they hear it or determined by the tone of the voice that delivers it. Human communication, even when talking about self-communication, is one of those subjects that goes very deep and is influenced by many factors. People communicate on a conscious as well as an unconscious level, and what is implied on a non-verbal level evokes a very impactful response. There are things that we may be aware of and totally unaware of, regardless of whether we are consciously aware of the impact words have on us or how much nuance and tonality and all the little details matter. So much of what is going on below the level of conscious awareness makes a tremendous difference and is very much in play regarding how we will react and behave.

Most of us believe that we carefully weigh out the pluses and the minuses, look at things, and use sound logic to reach a conclusion and decide which direction to take. Most people will tell you this is the process they go through, and it seems so real to them, and they are being totally honest when they tell you this is how they operate. Just about every decision we make as human beings is made on an emotional level, which has very little to do with logic and reason. Decisions are made in accordance with how we feel about things. Then we immediately turn around and try to justify that decision by more seemingly rational and logical (or, more accurately, pseudo-logical) methods, even to the point where they convince themselves this is what they were doing all along. Life moves along at a rapid pace, and much of it escapes us unless we slow it down so we can catch it in the moment.

The message I want you to come away with from this chapter is that what we say to ourselves is important. Equally important are the specific words we use in this conversation with ourselves. Many words seem to be synonymous; that is to say, they sound on the surface to mean the same thing. "I want to ride today" is not the same as saying, "I choose to ride today," and not the same as saying, "I will ride today." Sure, all three end up with you going for a ride, but the impact behind these words is quite different. Words do not merely transfer information. They hint at and affect us in sometimes dramatically different ways. Choose your words carefully, especially those you say to yourself, because you repeat them so often and because the implications and presuppositions underneath them affect us on an unconscious level. Even though you may not be consciously aware of their impact on you, when we accept them as they are, they do have a lasting effect on how we move through the world. Consider them carefully and revisit them to appreciate their importance fully. It can be a very useful practice to make a habit of delivering these goal statements or affirmations regularly. We repeat our suggestions to ourselves anyway. Doesn't it make sense to carefully craft what we say rather than haphazardly accepting and repeating these suggestions? It is probably most effective to deliver them after tapping into these affirmations while in a more hypnotic state, which I will speak about in a later chapter on self-hypnosis. The important thing is to carefully construct the statements you choose to incorporate into your belief system. Often begin the statement with the words "I am . . ." You want it to be present tense, not future tense ("I am going to . . ."). You want it in the "now," and if that is not yet ringing true, you can start the statement with the words "I am becoming . . ." or "I am beginning . . ." This implies you are acting now, and though not fully realized yet, the process is taking place now. To further clarify what I am getting at, you do not want to start by saying, "I am going to be . . ." because this is implying that tomorrow (or some future point in time), which is always putting things off into the future and if you ever heard the phrase "Tomorrow never comes" you might understand why I am belaboring this point. What you are doing is talking to the subconscious part of your mind, which takes things very literally, so trust me when I say it is important to talk using specific language because it is important. The other things you want to keep in mind are to make it something that is a little bit of a stretch but still very do-able, keep it in the "now," not the future, make it measurable and not ambiguous, give yourself a time deadline, and most importantly make it something that you believe you can do because if you tell yourself you will do something you do not believe you are not going to fool yourself. If you are not yet able to believe, as an example for someone afraid to ride their horse, a helpful goal statement might be "I am ready to ride my horse and will be back in the saddle before another month begins," or if you are not sure that you are ready, to begin with, "I am becoming ready to ride and will be back in the saddle on or before my next birthday passes." When you are feeling it is the right time for you (but certainly before your birthday), drop the word "becoming." Make your statement fit where you are, and at the same time, set a deadline, and do not let anything stop you from getting it done before that deadline.

Let me be clear that it is a very good idea to set a goal statement/affirmation and make it a habit to repeat it every day to condition it into your mind. Better yet, repeat it every time you pass through a doorway. It is even better to incorporate it into a self-hypnosis practice. When you access a trance state, it greases the wheels and allows these suggestions to sink in deeper and integrate more fully, which is useful. What is even more important in taking note of what you are saying to yourself day in and day out is that you are eliminating and replacing anything and everything that is taking you away from reaching your goal. Stop the negative self-talk, stop making yourself afraid, and replace those things with more useful things that take you closer to becoming the person you aspire to become. Everything I just said applies to the pictures you are making in your head. A daily visualization practice is a wonderful thing. Even more importantly, if you picture things that are not useful or make you afraid, hit the delete button and replace them with better things. When we do this repeatedly, we will be much further ahead than we would be if we continually allow ourselves to entertain thoughts that constantly scare us. What I am focused on here is getting you to understand how much what you see yourself doing and what you say to yourself genuinely matters. When we leave it all to chance, we will probably say many things that are detrimental to taking us to where we want to be going. Ask yourself often, is my thinking this way bringing me closer to or farther away from that self that I aspire to be? And then readjust accordingly. Monitoring self-talk is so useful and so effective and yet often so overlooked. When we pay attention to it and upgrade our language, we ultimately take control of our life's direction. Over time, a little at a time, the power of our self-talk builds and eventually steers our beliefs which lay the foundation and make it easy to choose where we end up going. You can take control of your life by choosing what pictures of yourself you make in your head and by what you say to yourself.

CHAPTER 6

Neuro-Linguistic Programming

Neuro-linguistic programming, or NLP, was first developed in the early seventies by a University of California, Santa Cruz linguistic professor, John Grinder, and his student, Richard Bandler. Neuro-linguistic studies the ways our thoughts affect our behaviors. It looks at how our brains interpret the signals they receive and how these interpretations determine how we behave. It helps us to understand how the language we use influences the way we think and the results we get. The techniques and strategies that Bandler and Grinder developed were based on the work of a handful of successful psychiatrists and therapists. At the time, the typical strategy employed by those working in the field of psychology was to focus on finding the root cause of the client's problem, hoping to find a solution. On the surface, this seems like a logical approach. If I can find out what caused the client to have this problem in the first place, then it may be possible to find the solution. If a person had a traumatic experience as a child and we can explore it and help them understand why they are now being triggered to feel upset or uncomfortable, they will be able to overcome these unwanted feelings. Unfortunately, in the real world, knowing why the problem started usually does not help the person to get rid of the unwanted feelings. If a person falls off their horse and becomes reluctant to ride again, remembering the experience that caused the fear does not help them get rid of it. Knowing the answer to the "why" question is not the same as knowing the answer to the "what to do about it now" question.

    I want to add a bit more on this topic before clarifying my beliefs concerning the need and effectiveness around the idea of searching for a root cause of a problem. There is a stark division among those of us who practice therapeutic hypnosis, and it winds us placing us in one of two camps. There are hypnotists whose go-to intervention revolves around finding the initial sensitizing event (ISE) and proceeding with what is known as regression therapy and those who believe there are better, more efficient ways of using hypnotic protocols to help an individual find the change they are after. Some hypnotists will use regression techniques with almost everyone who comes to see them, and others will never go there. Often those of us in the second group do not take our clients back in time for fear of retraumatizing them by bringing them back to a painful memory. Both sides of this tend to be very steadfast in their beliefs about the best, most effective approach. Although I am not in the group that you might refer to as being a regression hypnotist, and I rarely take this route with my clients, I believe there are certain times and situations when this is the best thing we can do with certain clients. In other words, although I do not search for the ISE to help those who come to see me, if a client brings it up and seems stuck where they are because of some specific trauma that they experienced in their past, I will address it because it seems obvious that until we deal with this experience, it may be difficult to move past it. In short, although I do not subscribe to the idea that we need to find the "why" before we can find a resolution, I have come to see that there are times when it may be the smartest card to play. Sometimes people will be giving you signals as to what they need; in these cases, ignoring what is being presented would be unwise. There is no one size fits all. People are complicated and there is no reason to make something simple harder than necessary. Now back to NLP.

Among those therapists who were most influential to the development of NLP practices were family therapist Virginia Satire, a very successful family therapist in California, Fritz Perls, the German psychiatrist who developed Gestalt therapy, and Dr. Milton Erickson MD, a medical doctor, a psychiatrist, and the person who many consider being the father of modern hypnosis. Bandler and Grinder examined and modeled what these therapists were doing with their clients that helped them achieve such extraordinary results and incorporated these ideas into NLP techniques and practices. The idea was that by modeling exceptional people, people who copy their behaviors and implement their successful strategies are likely to achieve similar results. If I follow the recipe that an accomplished chef uses, I should be able to bake a pretty good cake myself. Essentially, due to the influence of Milton Erickson, NLP incorporates a lot of hypnotic principles, protocols, and language. While hypnosis deals with the subconscious parts of our minds, NLP does a lot of similar things, but the focus tends to lean more toward the conscious aspects. In other words, while hypnotic work usually takes place after a trance state is induced, NLP is often done from a more conscious state. At times, I have described NLP as a more palatable form of hypnosis. By that, I mean that many people misunderstand what hypnosis is. Often, this comes from how hypnosis is portrayed in movies or from watching a stage hypnosis show. Some might come to believe that hypnosis is some kind of "woo-woo" form of mind control. They shy away from it, thinking of the dominant hypnotist exerting their will over the vulnerable subject. This is not at all what hypnosis is, but due to these misperceptions, NLP is often easier to accept and embrace than what they may think hypnosis is all about. Once a person understands NLP and hypnotic protocols, it becomes easy to see them being demonstrated throughout society in many different contexts, everywhere from television commercials, sales and marketing strategies, academic learning, and political dialogs. Many things now used in psychology, communication, and sales have come from the world of hypnosis and NLP.

Some of the things I use to help my "nervous-rider" clients overcome their reluctance to ride come directly from the world of NLP. Neuro-linguistic programming has been described as the modeling of excellence. Simply put, modeling is copying or imitating a person who is already successfully doing what you want to be doing well. This is the first way we learn to do anything in life. Before an infant can even speak, they watch their parents or those around them and copy what they are doing. This is the easiest, most natural, and most effective way we learn to behave. Have you ever noticed a baby watch their siblings or other little children around them and then shortly afterward attempt to copy the same behavior? When we get older, we may imitate a star athlete and try to move and shoot or run exactly like that person we look up to and want to be like. When I played baseball as a young boy, whoever came up to bat would declare, "I am number six, Mickey Mantle!" And the next batter might want to be Roger Maris or Willie Mays or whatever star that kid wanted to play like. This is a more useful way to advance our skills than we as children could have imagined. Someone who is accomplished and an expert in a particular skill set has already tried various ways to swing a baseball bat or a golf club. They have come up with the best way to swing that bat or club. If you mimic their physiology, posture, head tilt, pace, and the manner in which they move, then it is likely that it will also be an ideal way for you to move your body. Of course, you may find it useful to modify or tweak their physiology to feel even more comfortable, but it would be a very good position from which you can start.

It is also useful to copy a person who has had success on an emotional level as well. Suppose there is another equestrian at the barn where you ride, someone that you may look up to and want to model your riding abilities from their way of being, someone who seems to always be confident and composed whenever they are on their horse. Picture that person cantering or approaching a jump or doing whatever it is that you want to be doing. Picture yourself traveling through the world like them. What might they be feeling and thinking or saying to themselves that enables them to be able to carry themselves in a way that they seem so together and in control of themselves? This is exactly what modeling is all about. First, find a person that you emulate and wish to ride like. Watch them carefully as you can as they go about their business moving around and riding horses. Imagine what they may be thinking. What kind of things might they be telling themselves, and how might they feel in that moment? Then step into them and pretend that you are them and just go for it. Picture yourself as an actor who is playing the part of them and see yourself riding the same as they do. Allow yourself to daydream and play the part repeatedly until it becomes very familiar. Then, before you mount your horse, mimic their posture and/or tell yourself (much like we did back when we were playing baseball, pretending we were stepping into our idols), "I am being . . . [model's name]!" This body posture and saying will become associated with taking on their persona and anchoring in all the feelings that come with being them. If nothing else, doing all of this will take you out of whatever you would otherwise be thinking and saying to yourself that had made you afraid in the first place. Try this out and practice doing this regularly so that the next time you put your foot in the stirrup to start to ride, it will become your new, automatic default response. It is a very easy way to help you form new neurological pathways inside your brain.

Another useful NLP technique that I teach to my nervous-rider clients is what is called the "Magic Circle" or the "Circle of Excellence." Again, this is something that is practiced ahead of time repeatedly so that it becomes very easy and eventually will become your new automatic "go-to" process. Imagine placing a circle down on the ground in front of you. If you were to stand with a stick and scratch out a circle around you as you stand in the center, that is the size to make the circle. Think about how you want to feel whenever you go to ride. Maybe you call it relaxed or confident or composed or fearless or unstoppable. Pick out a color that you associate with the state that you want to step into. Picture the center of the circle as being that color. You might even picture the circle as a column going from floor to ceiling and see it as being filled with a vapor of that same color. Imagine yourself when you are feeling confident or fearless, or however you describe the way you want to be feeling.

As you begin building up feeling this way, step into circle and assume a powerful posture. Continue to build up the feeling, make the color brighter, breathe it in deeply, imagine it seeping into your pores, and see yourself growing larger and more powerful as you intensify the feelings you seek. Some people may even want to play a song in their head that pumps up those feelings that much more. When you feel completely immersed in the feelings, step out and carry those sensations with you. Play with this. I usually take people through this exercise while they are in a hypnotic state and then often give them an audio of the session so they can listen and relive the experience until it becomes fully integrated into who they are. Doing it this way makes it easy for them to step into the circle and automatically step into the powerful mental state that the process leaves within them.

One other NLP technique that some find helpful is called the Swish pattern. There are a variety of ways to do the Swish. Still, the one that I most often teach is to have the person picture themselves sitting on top of their horse, feeling, and looking (posture, facial expression, etc.) a bit anxious, nervous, or uncomfortable. Make the picture in black and white, a little fuzzy and unclear. Imagine taking that picture and placing it in a slingshot and, pulling it back, then letting it go. Watch it going out farther and farther, becoming smaller and smaller until it seems to disappear out in the horizon. Then as you loudly make the sound "SWISH," see the picture return fast, becoming bigger, brighter, and clearer than before. When it stops right in front of your eyes, see yourself confidently sitting on top of your horse with a smile on your face and head tilted as it would be when you are powerful, breathing slowly and deeply, and relaxed with the colors in the picture bright and clearly defined. Take a moment to allow all the feelings that come along with it to sink in, take a deep breath, shake it off, and repeat the process. Do this by replacing the picture of how you might now feel with one of you in your desired state and repeating the process about five or six times, going faster with each repetition. Your thoughts travel through your mind very quickly, and there is something about the speed at which you replace the unwanted picture with the new, desired image that adds to the power of the whole process. As you repeat it over again, it becomes easier to speed it up. This, and the sound of the Swish that you make, seems to drive the image into the deeper parts of your brain.

The last technique I want to include here is the meta pattern. Although this does not come from the original NLP strategies, I include this here. This comes from the work of John Overdurf, who has been practicing and training others in psychotherapy, hypnotherapy, NLP, and coaching for over four decades. I consider John somewhat of a grand mentor to me because he has trained many of my most influential mentors, including Melissa Tiers and Igor Ledechowski. John was trained in NLP by Richard Bandler and has taken what he found most useful from it and included many of his best practices, and developed HNLP, which stands for humanistic neuro-linguistic psychology. Here is how the meta pattern works. Most behavior is triggered by feelings that arise from the meaning we make, typically from either something we see or from something we hear.

For example, suppose when you are around another person, let's say it is your boss, and you start to feel inadequate, afraid, or even angry. Now perhaps on the surface, you might know why exactly this happens. You simply notice that often when you are around this person, this is how you begin to feel. First, go back to one specific time when this happened sometime in the past. Maybe it was the last time you were together or the last time you remember feeling this unwanted emotion. Now in your mind, slow the interaction down to explore and discover at precisely what point you first begin to have this particular feeling. You might be able to recall that it was the instant you heard their tone of voice or noticed that look on their face you started to get this feeling. What is probably happening inside your mind is that when you hear that tone or see that expression or gesture, you think it means something (they do not like the job I am doing for them). Instantly your brain releases neurochemicals into your bloodstream, which causes the sensations you begin to feel. All of this happens in the blink of an eye, which is why you need to slow down the exchange and pick up exactly what they do, which triggers your response. So now that we have the trigger, we want to let go of that feeling and think about how we want to feel instead of feeling inadequate (or afraid that if we do not please them, then we may not have the job anymore). So, at that point, instead of feeling the discomfort you usually experience whenever you are around your boss, you decide you would rather feel relaxed or even confident. Now, remember a time when you felt comfortable (in any setting). Recall all the details you can about how it feels to be in a truly confident state of mind. As you do this, that confident feeling will intensify, and as you are feeling this way, imagine hearing that tone in your supervisor's voice and notice how you are feeling about it now.

At this point, you want to go back and recall another time the tonality you heard from your boss or an expression that crossed their face made you feel uncomfortable. Think about how you would rather feel when you were around them, and this time suppose you come up with "I want to feel unbothered." You imagine what it feels like when nothing bothers you, and after you delve into that feeling and it builds up and gets stronger, imagine feeling like this and hearing that tone. You will probably not be as triggered by the tone. As you go through and repeat this pattern over and over again, you will begin to condition into your mind a new way of reacting to the trigger. Basically, you find the trigger. This is what the other person does, which sets off the chain that causes you to feel the way you no longer want to feel. Think about how you would rather feel instead. As you think about the resource state, it will build and intensify, and then while you feel empowered by being in this more resourceful state, think about the trigger.

The more you do this, the less powerful your reaction to the trigger will become until it no longer affects you the same way again. It is a very powerful way to change a reaction you no longer want to have. What we are doing with this process is recalling a specific time when something triggered an uncomfortable feeling inside us. This lights up the neural network of the non-resourceful state inside our brains. Then we carefully slow things down to find the exact moment we began to feel this unwanted sensation to reveal what triggered that response inside us. After we discover the trigger, we let go of the memory and the associated feelings and think about how we would rather be feeling instead by putting all of our attention on this new way of reacting, perhaps by remembering a time when we felt this way in some other situation. By doing this, the desired feeling will intensify, and while we are still feeling this way, we imagine how we might react differently to the trigger. Because the desired feeling is stronger in that moment, it will overpower and collapse the old unwanted feelings. Then we rinse and repeat, and it is the repetition that will break the pattern down even more until it becomes so weak that the next time the trigger presents itself, we will react differently.

People tend to treat us differently according to our state of mind when we engage with them. So much of how we are perceived is determined by how we are actually feeling. When you interact with a supervisor, boss, or client, you want to be coming from a place where you feel at ease and comfortable. If you feel anxious or inadequate whenever you are around a person, then they will not feel all that comfortable around you. This is because how we communicate with each other largely happens on an unconscious level. That is to say, what is really going on is often happening on a level below conscious awareness. It is not what we say as much as it is how we say it. It comes down to body language, which is mostly controlled by how we are feeling rather than how we want to be taken. A great deal of human communication takes place on an energetic level according to the vibe we are sending out. People pick up on this naturally, and to be congruent, we must be feeling it. You might be able to fool some of the people some of the time but to develop deep rapport or gain another person's trust. You must be genuine. Your true feelings will bleed through, and people will get a sense of who you are because it is for real and not forced.

Hopefully, you can make some progress by using the meta pattern by yourself. However, like many of the NLP patterns I have shared with you, it is probably easier to absorb, and you may gain more from having someone help facilitate the process with you, at least initially. Once you experience them for yourself and learn how to use them, you can certainly gain a great deal from doing them yourself. I have added them here because I know that they work. Like any hypnotic protocol, it is often more valuable to experience them in a deeper state of trance. Self-hypnosis can be every bit as powerful as experiencing a guided hypnosis session with a qualified hypnotist, but honestly, it is one of those things that becomes easier to do as you gain more experience. In effect, what you are doing can be thought of as trance training; in doing it over time, you are conditioning your mind to respond differently. The same can be said for mindfulness or meditation. Once you develop an ongoing practice, the gains will increase exponentially. Hopefully, you will be able to learn how to do all these things from reading a book, but admittedly it becomes a little easier to do when you enlist the help of an experienced practitioner.

CHAPTER 7

Hypnosis

So many misconceptions and misunderstandings come to mind for many people when the subject of hypnosis is introduced. Often people shy away from the idea of being hypnotized, believing that the subject relinquishes control and is left at the mercy of the hypnotist. Some think that strange unnatural mind control is taking place. Isn't it interesting that while mindfulness and meditation are accepted gateways into trance states, hypnosis is often seen as being some kind of woo-woo practice akin to witchcraft or voodoo?

Trance states are very normal and much more common than most people realize. It is my belief that people are walking around in a trance more often than not. It is the name we give to a state of focused attention. When we get engrossed in a book or a movie, we are in a trance state. When we find ourselves driving down a highway and realize that we are so lost in our thoughts, we cannot truly remember the last ten miles. Yet, our bodies automatically drove the vehicle without any conscious thought being given to it. It is because we were in a trance or what has been described as "highway hypnosis." We wash, shave, and get dressed every morning, thinking about what is on our to-do schedule later in the day. When we are in love, we seemingly do not notice anyone else in the room except the person who has captured our attention. When we drift off to sleep at night or slowly wake up in the morning and when we daydream while awake, we are dipping in and out of trance. When we are in a highly charged emotional state, whether it be anger or laughter, everything we think, do, or say is going to be affected by the state we are in at that particular time. The list goes on and on. You see, because of the way we are wired as humans, when we first learn to do something new, we must consciously focus on the steps we need to take to accomplish our objective. Once we learn the skill, our body seems to begin functioning automatically in order to complete the task, while our mind may be drifting off somewhere else. For example, when we first learn to drive, we must pay careful attention to how far we turn the wheel, press on the pedals, and stay vigilantly aware of what is happening in the roadway in front of us. After we learn to drive and have absorbed that learning, we might be singing along with the song on the radio, reminiscing about a memory that was evoked by the tune that is playing, chewing on a sandwich that is one hand, and scratching an itch with the other while steering with our knees and if something suddenly darts in front of our path without missing a beat we will instantly swerve or brake or both to avoid a collision. It is almost as if the car were driving itself, and although our attention was spread across half a dozen different things, so long as our eyes are on the road, we will react instinctively. People are in a trance of one sort or another for most of their waking hours.

What it all boils down to and why this is so useful is that the beliefs and programming that drive our behavior exist in the deeper parts of our minds. Some call it our subconscious or unconscious mind, and for this discussion, we will use those terms synonymously. Everything we learn and experience, all our memories and lessons and learnings, exist here in these deeper parts of our minds. By using hypnotic protocols, we can access and retrieve or readjust and change these programs to better suit our needs and desires. In other words, this is where we can reprogram those patterns and beliefs which are limiting us or enhance and empower those things that are already serving us well. We can remove the things that stop us and reinforce those things that can make us unstoppable. Hypnosis is the key that can unlock the doorway that opens us up to making the changes we need to make so we can more easily achieve our goals. This is not to say it is the only means by which to do all of these things, but it can be argued that it might be the safest, most effective way to make it as easy as possible for us to get whatever it is that we want.

To address things more pertinent to the subject matter of this book, let's look at what might be a typical scenario regarding a person who has a fear of riding their horse. It could be that the person had fallen off their horse and maybe they got hurt or avoided injury. Or perhaps they had an incident that frightened them and left them feeling vulnerable to being injured. Or maybe they just got caught up in a thought loop of what-ifs, and it took them down the path from bad to worse where now they have made themselves so scared they want no part of getting anywhere near the back of a horse ever again. The answer to the why question does not matter as much as it does to find the answer to the question of "What is it that they want?" and "How do we go about finding out how to accomplish this goal?" These are the more important questions that we want to find the answers to.

The question of what they want is highly personal, and only the individual themselves can give an honest answer. The only thing I can add would be that I can see from the position of an unbiased observer. For most people, a limited number of activities bring them true joy and pleasure in life. If you have plenty of fun and pleasure and do not need anything more, leave it alone. Sell the horse, move on, and spend your time enjoying whatever brings a smile to your face. But for those people who have discovered how much pleasure and happiness that being around and riding horses can bring into their life and have carefully considered what it is that they want, and after they have weighed out the pluses against the minuses and then realize what they want is to get back in the saddle again, it would be a shame to deny themselves the enjoyment that comes with being a horse-person. There is a lot of truth to the adage: "There is something about the outside of a horse that is good for the inside of a man!" I am certain that needs no explanation for those of us that know this to be true. The good news is that there are ways to overcome whatever might be stopping you right now. Whether your fears are real or imagined, you do not have to let them stop you. Life is just too darn short to talk yourself out of doing something that brings you joy. I am here to tell you that whatever happened or whatever you think might happen, there is no question that you can overcome and control your fears. I have seen enough people do it to know without a doubt that it can also happen for you.

The question remains, *how* do we help make that happen? The first step is to remove those thoughts which have turned into beliefs that are presently stopping you and then replace them with better thoughts, ideas, and beliefs that will allow you to get what you are after. This is where hypnosis proves to be so useful and valuable as being a means to that end. Hypnosis frees access to these deeper parts of the mind where the thoughts and beliefs may be keeping you stuck where you have been and allows you to open up to accepting helpful suggestions that enable you to see possibilities that might otherwise be hard to envision. There is probably no better methodology that can deliver the goods anywhere near as efficiently as hypnosis. By quieting the critical conscious parts of our brain down, which includes slowing down the brainwaves, one can better access the deeper parts of their mind because this is where the underlying beliefs and programs exist, which drive behavior. In my mind, there is no question that hypnosis is the quickest and most efficient means to achieve these ends. Without getting buried too far down into neuroscience, which supports this claim, what is happening is that working together, we can rewire the brain by replacing the existing neural pathways with new and improved ones. It is like putting a roadblock on a path through the jungle. When the trail we had always taken gets closed down, a new path will be blazed. Over time the more the new path is used, the clearer and more defined it will become. At the same time, the old path will become overgrown, and because vegetation grows quickly in the jungle, before long, the old pathway will be abandoned, and the new one will now become the road traveled. The brain grows very fast as well, and within weeks or, at most, a month or so, there will be a new default path that your thoughts will travel across. This means that the thoughts that are now causing a rider to hesitate or avoid riding their horse will fade away, and in their place, in very short order, new thoughts will embolden the rider, and a brand-new pattern of behavior will emerge. Change takes place in a few different ways, one being in an instant when an "aha" moment of clarity occurs. Another way change occurs is over time when, after repeating a new behavior, we gradually adopt it. Hypnosis and trance work speed up the process significantly, and because it happens on a level below conscious awareness, it seems effortless. There is no need to struggle internally, and any fighting with yourself will cease to be a problem.

It has been said that "All hypnosis is self-hypnosis," and there is more than a little truth in that statement. People can prevent themselves from going into hypnosis, and compliance is necessary for a successful hypnotic session to occur. The process is one of cooperative agreement, as no one can force you into a state of hypnosis. The only reason anyone would seek the help of a hypnotist is that it is easier to go into a hypnotic trance with the help of a trained hypnotist. This is certainly true, at least in the early stages of trance training. I refer to the learning curve as trance training because that is exactly what is happening. Just as a person learning to train their mind to go into a meditative state, it is more the same than different when it comes to hypnosis. When starting a meditation practice, many people find it difficult to shut off their minds and become frustrated. They tell themselves, "I just cannot do it," and often give up before they even begin. This is a shame because this is the nature of an untrained mind. Like a little kid that cannot be quiet and sit still, a person's "monkey mind" is hard to tune down at first. A meditative state and a hypnotic state are very much the same. What is happening inside the brain can be measured by a functional magnetic resonance imaging (fMRI) machine: the brainwaves slow down. These waves are measured in hertz and classified using the Greek alphabet symbols depending on the range they are measured at. The human brain at normal waking speed at which everyday conversation is measured is said to be in the Beta range. When they slow down to a more spacey daydream-like stage, they are classified to be in Alpha.

Slowing down further to a light sleep stage is referred to as being in Theta, then into rapid eye movement (REM), a deeper sleep range called Delta waves. Trance is never at a constant range and is not like an on/off light switch but acts more like a fluctuating dimmer switch. The difference between meditation and hypnosis has less to do with the state one's brain is in and more to do with what you do once you are in it. In meditation, people will access the state to wind down, enjoy the relaxation, and quiet the mind of the constant internal chatter that goes on incessantly; like sleep, this offers the mind and body an opportunity to restore, replenish and recuperate. Perhaps if one is contemplating a question, the silence might allow some insight to arrive. A person who engages in daily meditative practice can expect to become more laid back and relaxed, less stressed and hurried, and see better overall physical and mental benefits. Once a person understands the process around accessing a trance state and becomes acclimated to going into and being in a hypnotic state, much of the work can be done without the assistance of a hypnotist. This may not be true 100% of the time because it can be challenging to take on both roles of facilitator and subject simultaneously. But you can accomplish plenty by yourself using self-hypnosis protocols. Just as someone with a daily meditation practice can drop in very quickly and easily, the same is true for self-hypnosis. The state of mind is very much the same. The real difference is doing hypnosis is like doing meditation with a purpose or intending to accomplish some end by utilizing the trance state. Meditation may be practiced to enjoy peaceful restorative benefits or for spiritual purposes. Hypnosis is generally employed to eliminate unwanted behavior or amplify existing positive behaviors.

A person who engages in self-hypnosis regularly will see many beneficial outcomes and enhance abilities such as being better able to control their unwanted unconscious tendencies and re-program their mind to take them closer to becoming a version of themselves that they aspire to be, that is, their best self. Self-hypnosis is a more active way to engage rather than a more passive meditative practice. And by this, I mean you often engage in self-hypnosis with an agenda that you want to accomplish, usually removing a tendency towards behaving in a manner that does not serve you and/or strengthening a behavior that you want more of. Engaging in hypnosis facilitated by a hypnotist can often seem a bit more powerful experience for the subject. For many people, this seems to be a preferred way to develop and practice self-hypnosis because it is easier to remain focused and become comfortable with the state. After all, an experienced practitioner is directing you. Typically, when working with clients, the hypnotist wants to help their trance partner achieve whatever goals they have set up for themselves and often is willing to work with them as long as the client needs to achieve that end. Frankly, there is very little a person could not do on their own, but using the services of a skilled hypnotist makes things a whole lot easier, and there are some things you just cannot do all by yourself.

There are many ways to do self-hypnosis, and at the end of this book, links are provided to videos of a couple of different protocols that you may find helpful. What follows is a simple method that I use myself to access a trance state. In traditional hypnosis, you begin with an induction which can be seen as opening the door to trance, followed by a deepener, a process that invites the subject to go into an even deeper state. Then you do the "work," which can be as simple as a suggestion or involve one or a combination of techniques or processes to achieve whatever result you are looking for. After that, the client is brought back into a normal "waking" state. Now this is a very bare-bones explanation of what happens, but of course, there are a variety of intricacies that are often included to enhance the efficacy of the experience and the results. In this method of self-hypnosis that I am about to share, the introduction and the deepener are coupled together to streamline and speed up the process. This is to make things so easy and quick that it makes it easy for anyone to do it for themselves.

Let me add just a few more things before I continue. We take information in through our five senses; visual and auditory are the two most useful in effecting successful change work. Originally this process was taught to me when I went through my certification training to become a Mental Toughness Trainer and was framed as being a one-minute Mental Rehearsal Technique used to install a goal into the deeper part of your mind. You would start by writing down your chosen goal statement on an index card. The idea was that it was set up only to take one minute, and everyone has one minute, and by doing it five times a day in very short order because of the repetition spread out over time, you could easily condition it into your mind. The biggest problem with self-hypnosis is that it only works when you do it. If you neglect to do it, it will not work, and most people become distracted easily. Everyone wants results, but unfortunately, only very few will follow through and get them. Let me get on with explaining the technique. Start with your goal statement and write it in the present tense, not the future tense. It needs to be happening now, and it is often useful to start it with an "I am . . ." statement. Write out your goal, ensuring it is something within reach. It is not helpful to reach so far that a part of you might not believe it is possible to attain. Then begin the countdown:

"5 . . . I am beginning to feel relaxed."

"4 . . . Even deeper relaxed."

"3 . . . Relaxed . . . relaxed . . . relaxed."

"2 . . . Totally relaxed . . . and focused."

"1 . . . Focused like a laser beam."

Then, with as much emotion as you can muster, repeat your goal statement. Repeat until it feels right, and then allow the idea to sink in during the silence after the exhale of a deep breath. Then simply, count back up 1, 2, 3, 4, 5 using any language that seems helpful, or just count yourself back, and that is it. Do this five times each day until you know that you have it. Now this is how it was originally designed to be used, and it is quite an ingenious process in that it is short, sweet, and effective. And as mentioned, it is hard for someone not to do because it is so simple. The real secret is how you use your voice during the countdown. Go slow, taking at least enough time to allow for a deep breath in and out for each number. And it is helpful to use a hypnotic tone while you deliver the numbers. And what exactly is a hypnotic tone? That is how your voice sounds when you are in a trance. All of this may become clearer to you the more you play with doing this. And I will repeat once again that most would agree that it is a good idea to get a trained hypnotist to help introduce you to the trance state.

Trance is very natural and not uncommon, but most people do not recognize when they are in or out of trance. It is also a very distinct state that is easy to recognize once you become familiar with it. The more often you intentionally drop into trance, the easier it becomes to access it and recognize once you are there. It is a bit of a challenge to do justice in explaining it in written form, so I have set up a page for you on my website (listed at the end of this book) to go to so that you can listen to me demonstrate the process and download my voice counting you down. As is the case with all of this, I intend to show you exactly how to go into a trance state so that you can easily do it for yourself without my help. I am certain it will not take long to learn how to do it yourself. So what is going on here with this technique is that you are learning how to trigger your brain into going into a light trance state, which opens you up to become more ready to accept suggestions (your goal statement is a suggestion), or you can instead, create a movie inside your mind to run after the countdown has put you into a nice, light, hypnotic state. This movie can contain a highlight reel of memories that you had when you performed extraordinarily, or it could be a movie of you performing at the level of excellence that you aspire to live up to. In the context of why you are

Get Back on that Horse

reading this book, include memories of experiences that you had galloping your horse through an open field, feeling the freedom and adrenaline rush that comes with such a memory, or imagine yourself riding on a beach or over a jump or wherever you choose to do whatever you want to be able to do on horseback. Be creative, as you are the producer, the director, and the star, along with your horse of whatever movie you care to imagine. The key is to get the feeling that is evoked as you live out the scene. It is useful to get the body sensations involved in the exercise. Also useful is to allow and enjoy the afterglow in the silence after the action is finished.

I encourage you to take advantage of the downloads available to you and take a little time to learn how to do self-hypnosis. And if you are interested, a recommended reading list at the end of this book includes a book on self-hypnosis that will be more in-depth and offer more options than are listed here. Of course, you can enlist my help in getting you started, and this can make it easier and maybe more effective, but I realize that not everyone is comfortable with doing things this way, so at least try it out on your own and give it some time to play with it in order to do it justice. Hypnosis and self-hypnosis are useful practices and well worth whatever effort it takes to learn so you can incorporate them into your life. It should be taught to everyone at an early age. We have the most powerful computer ever created inside of our heads, but no one ever showed us how to properly operate it to get the most out of it. This is a big part of why we never tap into the tremendous power and resources we all have at our disposal. Your mind can be your most powerful asset or the very thing that is getting in your way of acquiring all the things you deserve to have in your life. Take the time and the opportunity to explore some of the possibilities that exist for you.

CHAPTER 8

Biological Response

While studying the work of Dr. Alan Goldberg (who influenced one of my mentors, Joni Neidigh), I could not help but notice the correlation between equestrians who have become unnerved and the underlying reason behind repetitive performance issues experienced by some competitive athletes. Sometimes, the traditional methods used by sports psychologists, like relaxation techniques, focus on positive self-talk, mental rehearsal, and concentration strategies, were just not enough to get an athlete back to good form. It is not all that uncommon for well-trained athletes who have spent years honing their skills to become frustrated when things just fall apart and their bodies seem to fail them, often at the most inopportune times. This may start when they are under a lot of pressure and cannot deliver and perform at their normal level. Then, depending on how they respond to it, it can devolve to the point where even their everyday performance begins to suffer. A pitcher who suddenly may lose control of their throwing arm and be unable to hit the strike zone, a diver who can no longer perform dives that were not even the most difficult in their repertoire or a basketball player who has trouble making foul shots or even an uncontested lay-up. In golf, it is so common that they have a name for it: the "Yips." This is when a player has so much anxiety that they cannot control the shaking in their arms. Even the slightest quiver can send even a relatively easy ten-yard putt off the mark, and this is a *condition* that can arise and affect golfers even at the tournament professional level. Perhaps the most famous case happened at the Olympics recently, when world-class gymnast Simone Biles could not compete because she suddenly became disoriented while doing mid-air maneuvers. What may be at play here is often the same thing happening to many of the thousands of equestrians who find themselves unable to enjoy the feelings that used to come whenever they put a foot in the stirrup and throw a leg over their horse. Sometimes, it is a biological response that cannot just be wished away but do not give up hope because it can be overcome in time and with diligent effort.

So, here is what may be happening. One of the primary functions, if not the most important function of the human mind, is keeping us safe from danger. The simple truth is that every one of us, as human beings, will at some point face some degree of trauma in our lives. This can be real or imagined, and it can be while riding our horse or anywhere else throughout our lives. It can be something we fear physically, like being injured, or something on the emotional plane, the embarrassment we feel because we think people are talking about and judging us. This is a very real fear for many people and may have a serious impact on their behavior. The thought of other people laughing about us behind our backs is enough to freeze people, leaving them unwilling to take that risk. Many people admit to being more afraid to speak in public than they are afraid of death. So, regardless of what might seem logical, the reality is that if you build something up in your head to be that big of a deal, then it is a big deal, and so it becomes a very real threat to you. I will use examples that follow in the context of riding, but the trauma we experience in any area of our lives can bleed out and manifest itself in an inability to ride. This can begin with a major trauma (with a capital "T"), like if we were to take a very bad spill from our mount and perhaps get injured or witness or even just hear about a catastrophic event suffered by another rider and then imagine ourselves going through a similar experience. Often, it can be an accumulation of many less severe (small "t") traumas. These traumas are stored in our being, sometimes as memories, even though we may not be consciously aware of all of them. It can be as innocuous as something we saw in a movie or read in a book that we hardly paid all that much attention to at the time but could still be retained and stored deep in our psyche. This is why it may be so frustrating when you and your trainer or coaches cannot figure out why you cannot do things at the same level you once were able to perform at. When you have had a major injury, it can be easy to answer the "why" question, but this is not always the case because the experiences that were unconsciously checked off as being potentially dangerous to our well-being were not things that had an obvious connection to us at all.

We know that a part of our brain, the amygdala, is triggered whenever we perceive a threat or danger that could

Get Back on that Horse

harm us. And when activated, the fight, flight, or freeze response is triggered. I have not minimized the fact that there is some degree of danger that we all face if we decide to spend our time around horses. It is by far not the most dangerous thing we do, and the argument can certainly be made that it is far more dangerous driving in a car to the barn than riding on our horse. But, as I said, trauma, real or imagined, is stored, and it does accumulate and get to the point where it can reach its limit, overwhelm us and activate the amygdala. So, if there is no one to fight (except us), and if we are worried about what others will think of us and running away is not a feasible option, all that is left is the freeze response. When our amygdala is triggered, and we push ourselves past our comfort level and try to muscle through it, then it will likely be the freeze response that kicks in. It may be that we become short of breath and our muscles tighten up, or depending upon the degree of activation (think dimmer switch rather than on/off light switch), we might find ourselves shaking uncontrollably, or those muscles may lock up and shut down completely. We find ourselves unable, through the force of our will, to restore the capacity for them to function. All this makes one susceptible to a panic attack, and none of it is conducive to an enjoyable or safe ride. Everything is happening on a biological level, which is to say our survival mechanism has been triggered, so we no longer have much control at that moment. So, where does this leave us?

On the surface, it might all sound a bit hopeless, but remedies are available. The key is to become aware of the early signs that you are beginning to become activated. This means knowing what the first signals for you are. The first sign could be a change in breathing, or it could be you start to talk yourself into anxiety, thinking about bad outcomes or "What if" scenarios. Maybe you start running movies in your head, which scares you, or perhaps the feeling of tightness in your muscles or nervous energy running through your veins. All of these are signs, and the order in which they appear differs for everyone. Pay attention to your thoughts and your body sensations. Find out what happens first and try to pay attention to these things so that as soon as you notice them, you can back off and remain safe. Remember, it is all about the perception of danger that activates the amygdala, so we must stay within the boundaries of what we feel safe with. So whatever safe means to you is your starting point. If that means do not ride any faster than a walk, or it means do not ride outside of a small paddock or even a lunge pen, or if this means that the only way for you to restore your sense of safety is to have someone put a lead line on the horse and walk alongside you and lead you around the riding ring, then this is where you start. Wherever it is that you feel safe is where you start. Do not worry because as you go forward, this zone will expand.

Of course, no experienced rider wants to be seen in public being led around a round pen like a kid on a pony ride. Do what you must do to figure out the logistics. Ride in off hours at times when there are not a lot of onlookers around. If it is important for you to overcome these limitations and slowly regain the ability to ride again fearlessly or at least be able to handle yourself on the back of a horse. This will be different for everyone, so it is up to you to pay close attention to those subtle signs that overactivation may be starting and then do whatever it takes to stay for you to continue to feel safe. If that entails taking baby steps initially, then this is what you need to do. As I said, you will probably progress much faster than you think. Hypnosis can really help speed up your progress. You may be able to conquer your fears and anxieties all on your own, but depending on where you are at with all of this, the better choice may be to seek the help of a professional.

Another thing for you to consider is that many people think they are concealing their fears from the rest of the world and are most likely fooling anybody. Those busybodies in the peanut gallery who are watching closely and are quick to judge or gossip are not worth expending your energy to worry about. When we are brave enough to stand up and confront our fears and decide to tackle them head-on, they may seem a lot less daunting. And don't be too surprised when you change your behavior to notice those around you also begin to change how they treat you. The truth is that many people who are busy judging and gossiping about others do so only because they have their own issues with feeling safe while riding. It is not uncommon that they may be attacking you to deflect attention away from themselves and their own insecurities. People pick up on another person's energy. They might be picking up on the signals you are unconsciously sending out and will begin to treat you accordingly. It will show when you decide to stop caring what other people think or say about you. Decide to stop caring about what others are thinking about you, and then do it. If you believe that you cannot do that on your own, then get help. For the most part, most of what you are telling yourself they must be thinking is all in your imagination because most people are too busy worrying about themselves to have much time worrying about anyone else. Letting go of the worry over what others might think will be the most useful and freeing thing you could ever do for yourself.

If any of what we have been discussing in this chapter sounds familiar and you decide to try to tackle this problem on your own, there are a few more things that would be useful for you to be aware of. First, you must become conscious of exactly what you are saying to yourself and begin to monitor these thoughts. It is hard, if not downright impossible, to stay positive all the time. Confidence, like any state, is always going to fluctuate, and there will be moments of doubt that will surface. Keep in mind that there is a negativity bias that we all are predisposed to, which comes from our survival mechanism. Constantly searching for danger is a large part of what has kept us safe for generations. It is part of our nature, and for the most part, it serves us well. This becomes problematic when we find ourselves caught in a situation constantly triggered by "what if" thoughts over imagined threats. Two things are likely to happen when a person's threat response has been repeatedly activated. The amygdala often remains in a potentiated state (a fancy way to say hair-triggered state), at least in the short term. If you ask an electrician, they will tell you that the more a circuit breaker trips, the less it takes to trip it again. That happens when a person is subjected to repeated or severe response activation. The other thing that happens is that as soon as the person begins to feel aroused, they immediately start to worry even more about a recurrence of past unwanted feelings and behaviors. This worry response will add more fuel to the fire. So, whenever you first notice the early signs of becoming activated, it will often be a combination of destructive thought loops along with some physical sensations.

Take your attention off your thoughts and put the focus solely on the physical sensations. Become curious about them. Will they move around? Will they intensify, stay the same, or decrease? These sensations are caused by a release of neurochemicals into the bloodstream, and they always decrease eventually. They always go away without fail, usually within 30 to 60 seconds. The only thing that keeps them going is ruminating. This is why it is so helpful to focus on the body sensations these thought loops are causing. By becoming fascinated by what you are feeling, it will then repeatedly interrupt the tendency of those thoughts. When you stop the thoughts, it will cause the sensations to recede and quickly disappear altogether. Many people walk around feeling anxious and easily bothered most of the time only because they are perpetuating the release of neurochemicals into their system by thinking thoughts that are keeping them in a state of fear. If you focus on the physical sensations, you will not be thinking scary thoughts. Notice those body sensations; do not fight them, just allow them to be there and get curious to see what they will do next.

Another thing you can do to get yourself out of your head is to pick out something in your environment that catches your eye, study it, and then describe it to yourself in detail. The more you focus on it and the greater detail you use to describe it, the better. Again, this does two things. First, it takes you out of your thinking, including those thought loops that will only continue to scare us into thinking we might be in danger. And second, if you are aware that your environment is free of anything that will harm you, you will begin to believe you are safe. After you explore one thing in your visual field, pick out another and repeat the process as many times as you want. You want to interrupt the pattern of overthinking and keep yourself from falling into the trap of incessant rumination. As I mentioned, human beings tend to lean towards having a bias towards negative thinking and are left to their own devices. We will do this unless we consciously try to disrupt the pattern by placing the focus elsewhere, whether that be what our body is feeling or different objects around us. These things I am sharing with you can prove helpful in countering anxiety in any situation. And how we label things has a great deal to do with how we experience them.

What is the difference between the physical body sensations we label as being anxiety and those we call excitement? Suppose you recall and compare two experiences, one where you felt anxious and the other when you were what you called excited. In that case, you might realize that the physical sensations you have felt in these two situations were very similar, if not identical. Two different people might walk into a room full of strangers gathered at a social event, and one may say they are excited while the other feels what they call anxiety. They might feel very close to the same physical sensations and label them very differently. Labels are emotionally loaded and carry strong connotations that impact how we meet an experience. What may be true is that when we expect a positive outcome, we will label the sensations we are feeling as excitement. When we go into a situation imagining things might not go well, we feel what we call anxiety. The bottom line is that our thoughts and expectations and the meaning we make about what we are about to experience have more to do with how we feel than do the actual physical sensations themselves. Knowing this, it might be wise to take care of how we label things as well as the meaning we make about what is happening. Sometimes, the easiest thing we can do is interrupt the thoughts, causing the release of neurochemicals that are causing the body sensations in the first place. It really can be that easy to allow us to experience what happens around us in a completely different way.

CHAPTER 9

Choices

Judy had always loved to ride, whether it was in the arena or out on the trails. Riding her horse had always been her go-to stress-relieving strategy. It had been close to a year since she had the challenging experience. Her horse, Hanna, a flashy strawberry roan mare with a blaze and white stockings all around, had been up on her toes right from the start. It was a cool autumn afternoon in the northeast, and the wind had picked up a bit, which caused the barnyard to come alive with movement. Hanna had her eyes wide open, on alert for anything and everything that might be threatening. After tacking her up, Judy pointed her mount towards the stable gate, which led out to the wooded trails. She wasn't sure if it was something blowing in the wind or an imaginary boogeyman that set the little mare off, but ten steps down the bridal path were all it took for the mare to become unglued and tuck her chin and take off on a dead gallop. Judy had a lifetime of experience being around horses and had been reading the signs that her horse was on edge, so it wasn't as if it were a surprise that something like this might happen. She grabbed up some rein and talked to her mount in a futile attempt to settle her down, but Hanna was having none of it, and despite Judy's best efforts, the horse was too far gone and completely overtaken with panic. It wasn't until the horse swerved left, unexpectantly causing Judy to lose a stirrup, that the rider became worried. They continued down the lane like this for quite some time before Judy was able to finally right herself in the saddle, regain some semblance of control and pull the little horse to a stop.

Although it wasn't pretty, Judy had done a pretty good job staying on and riding out the excitement, and in the whole scheme of things, it could've gone much worse, but for those few critical moments, it was those feeling of helplessness that consumed Judy which particularly shook her. This wasn't her first rodeo ride, and over the years, she had experienced much worse, but for some reason, the incident left her filled with uncertainty and doubt that was unlike anything she had ever felt before while riding. She kept a tight rein on Hanna as they retraced the steps and returned to the barn. A few other riders out on the trail that day witnessed what had just happened, which added to Judy's insecurities. Although she knew there was not much else she could have done under the circumstances on top of everything else, she felt inadequate and knew that she probably looked more than a little foolish. Regardless of what the others may have been thinking, this is how Judy felt inside. When they rode up to the barn, Judy felt a big sigh of relief to dismount, and she went about putting the horse away for the day.

As the days passed after this incident, Judy had a hard time forgetting what had happened. The more she thought about it, the more she tended to make it worse in her mind by thinking about all the "what-ifs" that could have happened to make things worse. She ruminated incessantly for the days and weeks that followed. Every time she played the scene out in her head, the danger seemed more imminent, and the uncomfortable anxiety in the pit of her stomach grew stronger. By the time she dragged herself back to the farm, she had no desire to saddle up her mare and ride. This went on for weeks that turned to months, and it soon became the norm that Judy would show up with a few carrots, brush and groom her horse for a while, and then on some occasions, take her in the round pen and lounge her to get her some exercise before finding a good excuse not to climb onboard. After all, winter was setting in, and the weather was not all that nice to ride anyway. Judy tried to overlook that she never seemed to have time in her schedule to show up on a good day when the sun was shining. After a while, it became hard for her to ignore that she only went to the barn on days when it was too cold, windy, wet, or just too much for her to be able to ride. This went on for months on end and after a while, Judy had a pretty good suspicion that this pattern had not gone unnoticed by the other ladies in the barn. As time passed, one by one, they just stopped asking Judy if she wanted to join them on a ride. The litany of excuses of a headache or the weather or her back pain had flared up again seemed never-ending, and it became obvious to everyone exactly what was going on.

Judy knew that they all knew what was happening, and she now showed up at the barn feeling sheepish, still trying to put on a good face and pretend that nothing had changed. It was tough on her, though, because this behavior was incongruent with who Judy had always seen herself as being. From her early teens onward, she was always consumed with a passion for riding. Back then, there was no such thing as the weather being too bad to go out for a ride. Put a rain slicker on when it was pouring or a ski hat and gloves when it was snowing. Back then, there was nothing that would stop her. She had always thought of herself as a horsewoman. This is how her friends and family saw her, this was how she saw herself, and this is who she is. That seemed to be the toughest part of all of this. When a person so firmly identifies with being someone and then suddenly, this is no longer true, well, it just leaves them with a feeling that goes beyond inadequate. It left Judy feeling lost. Who was she now that she was no longer an experienced and hard-core equestrian? This, more than anything, left her feeling confused, uncertain, and totally rattled. And it is not like she could share any of this with anyone. She pretended when she was around her friends and her children that nothing had changed and that all was well. When her husband asked her how things had gone at the barn that day, Judy told him everything except that she did not ride that day, that week, or that month. After all, her mate knew very well how much money Judy was spending, and who knows how he might react if she told him anything about any of this. Nope, Judy did not tell a soul. How could she? She was not ready to admit the truth even to herself. She just kept all of this, all of her feelings, bottled up inside.

Now, none of this is a good idea, and none of it is wise, and none of it would ever be recommended, but this is exactly what most of us would do. How often have you tried to ignore a situation that makes you uncomfortable, hoping that it might suddenly and spontaneously just solve itself? We all do stuff like this, whether it is a relationship issue or a health issue, or a mistake that we make. How many of us just want to bury our head in a pillow, hoping when we open our eyes, it will just go away and disappear, and somehow everything will just go back to "normal"? This is what we do as human beings being human. Until we learn that this simply does not work, we tend to do this as our first impulsive strategy. Very few of us will do anything much different until we learn; most of what we learn is through doing things the hard way. That is to say, most of us learn by making our own mistakes, not from the mistakes of others, and rarely from listening to the advice of others. I know this is how I have learned most of what I know. It is just the way it is. Our teachers try to tell us, and our parents and our friends all try to tell us but let's face it, most people need to make their own mistakes and then feel the pain from the consequences, and then eventually, we learn. And if we don't learn right away, it is a pretty good bet that life will unfold in a brand-new way to give us another chance to learn the lesson it is trying to teach us.

This is exactly how things played out for Judy. The status quo continued until, eventually, the discomfort got to be too much for her to deal with. And after enough time went by, Judy decided that this was just no longer going to fly. This was not who she was, and this was no longer going to be who she was any longer. Enough was enough, and it was time for a change. Discomfort, unpleasantness, and pain are a gift that builds up until we are driven to take action to stop them. And this is where Judy was at this point. She had had enough and could no longer pretend, could no longer ignore, and could no longer stand it. She had no idea how she was going to do it. She was not even sure she could ever overcome her fear and return to where she was. All she knew was that she was no longer going to continue doing what she had been doing, and although she had no idea how things would work out, she knew that she was not going to keep being who she had been for the last ten months any longer. And that was the day, the moment things began to change—the moment she chose to decide to do and be something different.

When I first met Judy, I knew she would get what she was after. I knew before she did that she would succeed. I could see she was ready. I knew it because she was here. She had taken the hardest step, the first step. I knew that she had found her why, and even though she did not yet know the answer, just the fact that she found her why was enough to get her started. Now, I did not know when she would get there, and I had no idea how long it might take her. All I knew was that as long as she kept at it, she would succeed sooner or later. There is an old saying about failure: It is impossible to fail unless you stop trying. Think about it. As long as you keep going, if you come up short, all you did was learn another way that did not work. Just ask Thomas Edison about this. As long as you keep taking the next step, there is no such thing as failure, and you will surely get there.

Judy did not have to tell me much about her story. I did not need the details because they were unimportant. All I needed to know was where she was headed, and that was all she needed to know as well. Of course, she did not know anything for sure. She just needed the intention and the commitment to carry on to fruition. So long as she had this, things would work out satisfactorily for her. And things did work out beyond whatever expectations she may have held when she began. Judy is now back riding her mare regularly, enjoying herself again without the anxiety or the worry that stopped her for all those months. And her satisfaction goes well beyond the pleasure she gets when she finds herself traveling through the woods or the freedom she feels when she goes cantering across a field. And it no longer makes any difference what the weather outside happens to be. The real satisfaction comes from the accomplishment of letting go of the stories that held her prisoner to her own thoughts once and for all. The real freedom and the real peace come from knowing that she is back in control of her thoughts, emotions, and behavior.

Now I am not about to take the credit for what Judy has been able to do because she is the one who did what it took. I did not do much of anything other than walk alongside her for a short time while she found her way. I knew she would get there. I have seen it before. I have a pretty good idea of what is possible because I know just how powerful people can be. The power is within them; all it takes for them to see it for themselves is to let go of the stories that have been stopping them. Once they open themselves up to possibility, it is only a matter of time before they succeed. It really is that simple. And sure, hypnosis helps make it easier, and sometimes we might stumble upon the tool or technique that might make a difference, but the power comes from within them.

I am hopeful that you found some things within this book that proves helpful for you going forward, whatever journey you happen to be on. At the end of this book is a list of books you might care to read and links to some supplemental videos that can better show you how to do some of the exercises described within. Judy and countless others have been able to turn things around and overcome the obstacles stopping them, and you can as well. Believe this because it is true. It all starts with making a choice. No one else can do it for you. Decide for yourself, and whenever you are ready to act, go for it and don't look back. Keep going. No one needs to stay stuck in a place that keeps them from being exactly who they are here to become and from doing everything they choose to do.

Resources

Aka Margaretha Montagu, and Margaretha de Klerk. *Horse Riding Confidence Secrets*. Independently Published, 2018.

Andrea Monsarrat Waldo. *Brain Training for Riders*, 2016.

Cooper, Emma. *The Nervous Horse Rider's Handbook*, 2021.

Fader, Jonathan. *Life as Sport*. Da Capo Lifelong Books, 2016.

Haime, John. *Ride Big! : The Ultimate Guide to Building Equestrian Confidence*. North Pomfret, Vermont: Trafalgar Square Books, 2021.

Lyons, John. *Lyons on Horses*. Doubleday, 2010.

Marion, Jess. *The Hypnotic Coach*, 2021.

Nongard, Richard. *The SEVEN Most EFFECTIVE Methods of SELF-HYPNOSIS*, 2019.

Rollnick, Stephen, Jonathan Fader, Jeff Breckon, and Theresa B Moyers. *Coaching Athletes to Be Their Best*. Guilford Publications, 2019.

Selking, Dr. *Winning the Mental Game: The Playbook for Building Championship Mindsets*, 2022.

Stewart, Daniel. *Braver, Bolder, Brighter : The Rider's Guide to Living Your Best Life on Horseback*. North Pomfret, Vermont: Trafalgar Square Books, 2021.

———. *Pressure Proof Your Riding - Mental Training Techniques to Gain Confidence*. J.A. Allen & Co Ltd, 2013.

Tiers, Melissa. *The Anti-Anxiety Toolkit : Rapid Techniques to Rewire the Brain*. New York: Center For Integrative Hypnosis, 2011.

Tripp, James. *Hypnosis without Trance*. Real Magic Media, 2021.

Williams, Moyra. *Understanding Nervousness in Horse and Rider*. J A Allen & Company Limited, 1990.

Thank you for reading my book!

If you enjoyed this book and would like to help other people find it too, please post a review on Amazon. Thank you.

Thomas Mulryne is available to speak at your upcoming event.

You can reach him through one of his websites:

www.MentalSportsCoach.com

www.EquestrianHypnocoach.com

www.GetInZone.com

Printed in Great Britain
by Amazon